WHAT IS TRUTH?

Dr Peter Vardy is Vice Principal of the University of London's Heythrop College where he lectures in the Philosophy of Religion. He is author of the best-selling Puzzle series of books now translated into six languages. In Australia he acts as a consultant in Religious and Values Education to schools, including Geelong Grammar School and Melbourne Grammar School, and has been responsible for introducing into Australia the Five Strand Approach to Religious and Values Education.

WHAT IS
TRUTH?

Peter Vardy

John Hunt
Publishing Limited

Copyright © 2003 John Hunt Publishing Ltd
46A West Street, Alresford, Hants SO24 9AU, U.K.
Tel: +44 (0) 1962 736880 Fax: +44 (0) 1962 736881
E-mail: office@johnhunt-publishing.com
www.johnhunt-publishing.com

Text: © 1999 Peter Vardy

Formerly published under the title *What is Truth?* by the
UNSW Press, Sydney, Australia and reprinted in 2000.

This reissue: 2003

Cover painting: 'The Escape' by Norman Parker, 1997

ISBN 1 84298 100 5

A CIP catalogue record for this book is available from
the British Library.

Printed in the U.K. by Ashford Colour Press

NEW COLLEGE LECTURES
AND PUBLICATIONS

New College is an Anglican college affiliated with the University of New South Wales, Sydney. In 1986 the college set up a trust to conduct an annual series of public lectures. The lecturer is asked to take up some aspect of contemporary society and to comment on it from the standpoint of their Christian faith and professional experience. The inaugural lectures were given in 1987 by Professor Malcolm Jeeves of St Andrews University, Scotland, and in subsequent years lecturers have come from Australian and overseas universities, as well as the wider community.

1987   Prof Malcolm Jeeves (University of St Andrews, Scotland)
        Minefields, Lancer Books (ANZEA), 1994.

1988   Dr Veronica Brady (University of Western Australia)
        Can These Bones Live? Federation Press, 1997.

1989   The Hon Keith Justice Mason (NSW Supreme Court)
        Constancy and Change, Federation Press, 1990.

1990   Prof Stanley Hauerwas (Duke University, USA)
        After Christendom? ANZEA, 1991.

1991   Prof Geoffrey Bolton (University of Queensland).

1992   Prof Peter Newman (Murdoch University, Western Australia).

1993   Prof Robin Gill (University of Kent, England)
        Beyond Self Interest, New College, 1993.

        Rev Dr John Polkinghorne, KBE, FRS (Queens' College, Cambridge)
        Religion and Current Science, New College, 1993.

1994   Prof Geoffrey Brennan (Australian National University).

1995   Rev Dr John Polkinghorne, KBE, FRS (Queens' College, Cambridge)
        Beyond Science, Cambridge University Press, 1996; Polish ed, 1998; Greek ed, 1999.

1996   Les Murray (Australian poet)
        Killing the Black Dog, Federation Press, 1997.

1997   Dr Elaine Storkey (London Institute for Contemporary Christianity, England)
        Constructed or Created: The Great Gender Debate Paternoster Press/UNSW Press, 2000.

CONTENTS

Part 3
THE CENTRE CAN HOLD

FOREWORD

When Peter Vardy addressed the audience during the 1998 New College Lectures in Sydney, he indicated that one of his goals for his series of lectures on *What is Truth?* was to 'disturb'. And disturb he did! No other series of lectures has engendered greater debate within the College throughout their 12 year history.

The New College Lectures provide an opportunity for a reputable scholar to take up some aspect of contemporary society and comment upon it from the standpoint of their Christian faith and experience. Peter Vardy from Heythrop College at the University of London is widely recognised as a philosopher and one of the leading figures in religious and values education in Britain. He is therefore well placed to address the age-old, yet forever contemporary question of the nature of truth with professional competence and passion. As an Anglican who works in a Jesuit college and who has been chair of the governing body of Britain's second oldest Methodist school, his Christian faith and experience is distinctly ecumenical.

What is Truth? was a challenging series of lectures. Peter Vardy has now transformed them into an equally challenging book. I for one have been 'disturbed' by Peter's text and have had to examine afresh some of my own beliefs and assumptions. In many ways, however, this has proved to be a very helpful and positive experience. I still have a long way to go and I am sure that I will return to this book again and again as I seek to understand my beliefs and convictions about truth.

This is not to say that I am convinced by Peter Vardy at every point. Far form it! We must all make up our own minds on issues as important as this. Peter Vardy's ideas, however, are now before us and we as readers have the freedom to judge his interesting and sometimes controversial views.

The New College Lectures have a proud history and the list of previous lecturers and publications is impressive. The lectures are delivered within the academic context of the University of New South Wales, and the lecturers are given freedom to handle the agreed topic as they choose. The views they express are not necessarily those of New College.

Peter Vardy and this publication make their own unique contribution and are worthy additions. It is fitting that this book is the first in what hopefully will prove to be a long series of publications by UNSW Press.

The trustees thank Peter Vardy for a splendid series of lectures and thank Robin Derricourt and Nada Madjar from UNSW Press for their assistance in publication.

Allan Beavis
Master, New College
University of New South Wales

DEDICATION AND ACKNOWLEDGMENTS

Some people are convinced that they have the truth and are anxious
to ensure others also have it. These are the fundamentalists.
Some people spend their lives in distractions and activity and are
indifferent to the truth.
Some people deny there is any truth and devote their life to this
denial.
Others construct their own truths or at least come to understand
the forces that have constructed the truths by which they live.
A few, however, seek the Truth and knowing they will never find it
in its entirety, stake their lives on trying to live it. It is to this latter group that this book is dedicated.

I would like to thank my friends and colleagues who have read
specific sections and have helped to correct errors. These include
Catherine Cowley, Roger Dawson, Peter Gallagher, Judy Grill, Jeremy
Hall and Vaclav Umlaf. The remaining errors are all my own. The
editor of this book, Nada Madjar, has been patient, kind and helpful
throughout the process of putting this book together. I have been
fortunate to have had such generous help and am very grateful to
her. I would also like to thank the Trustees of New College, University of New South Wales in Sydney, who invited me to give the 1998
New College Lectures on which this book is based. I am particularly grateful to Allan Beavis, the Master of New College, and his staff
for their kindness when I was with them.

Peter Vardy — University of London

PART ONE

WHAT IS TRUTH?

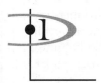

THE IMPLICATIONS OF A DENIAL OF TRUTH — OR THE CLAIM TO HAVE IT

> Are we like little boats, anchors adrift with no steering,
> no meaning and no purpose?
> Little groups of boats get together and anchor to any bit
> of flotsam and hang onto it and say 'This is it'.

In countless classrooms around the Western World, young people are taught tolerance, openness to alternative perspectives, to value themselves and their own views and to accept and revel in diversity. All this is praiseworthy, but it carries with it a very real danger which seems clearly at work within society. There is a radical relativism amongst many young people who have in some cases come to see truth as a dirty word. This radical relativism is no accident. The intellectual origins are the result of a long philosophic process, not least the impact of post-modernism which sees truth in all fields as radically perspectival and the search for any ultimate truth as folly.

In this book I want to try to defend the search for truth and, by implication, the claim that in the field of education there is a need to reintroduce a curriculum which takes the search for truth seriously. Unless there is truth to be sought, the distinction between truth and untruth becomes meaningless. That which is generally accepted is taken as real and true, and the idea of what is ultimately real becomes a chimera. This is highly dangerous politically, philosophically, socially, environmentally and personally. In the absence of a search for truth, the most powerful influence on young people is the media and the world of appearance. With the increased influence of the media and the increased concentration of media power, young people are never left alone — television, radio, music and popular culture bombard them with images. Advertisers seek to persuade and to create desires and hopes which they would not otherwise have. Politicians manipulate their perceptions of the world and the idea of achieving some sort of truthful appraisal of the human condition seems doomed. Indeed, many today would argue precisely that ultimate truth is folly.

In the face of a culture in which truth is seen increasingly as a dirty word, there seem to be no firm landmarks, no points that can hold sure and unchanged in a sea of relativity. One person's view seems as good as any other, leaving the door open for people to believe in anything. One of the consequences of this is an increase in the popularity of religious cults. Also, millions of people in the United States firmly believe that unidentified flying objects and aliens frequently visit this planet. At the same time, religion is seen either as increasingly irrelevant, a minority activity which is tolerated because it is harmless or else is being taken over by increasingly strident voices.

In the face of all these factors, I want to put forward a case for truth, perhaps even for 'Truth' with a capital 'T'. However, I also want to challenge those religious groups which claim in a strident voice to have *the* truth. They are to be found in many fields as well as in more extreme forms around the world. I will argue that their lack of modesty and humility, their seeming lack of awareness that they may be wrong, is radically misguided. In too many cases around the world fundamentalism is on the rise and few either dare or are willing to stand against it. Sadly, in the Western World many responsible churches, or parts of them, are being hijacked by those convinced that only they have access to the Truth and everyone else is wrong. It is not easy to persuade them otherwise, as Thomas Merton recognised:

> It is relatively easy to convert the sinner, but the good are often completely unconvertible simply because they do not see any need for conversion ... What matters then is to cultivate this quality of acceptance in a sociological milieu and then ... even objectively unjust works can be counted virtuous and Christian, since they are approved by those who are locally certified as 'good' ... Truly the great problem is the salvation of those who, being good, think they have no further need to be saved and imagine their task is to make others 'good' like themselves![1]

This book is partly intended to resist such people. Felipe Fernandez-Armesto provides a good definition of fundamentalism:

> Fundamentalism means uncritical, literal acceptance of what are supposed to be the founding doctrines or documents of a tradition. It demands a closed mind and the suspension of rational faculties; it is attractive only to the desperate and the dim. The huge allegiances it commands are proof of the strength of the reaction against relativism, evidence of the revulsion people feel from the prospect of a truthless universe. Its power to reassure is irresistible to its adherents and repulsive to everyone else. For people who I recognise as religious, it is the very negation of religion, for doubt is a component of faith and reason a divine gift which only devilish inducements can make you forego.[2]

I am a philosopher and philosophers traditionally have been held to have a passionate interest in truth. Today this interest appears to have waned and the search for wisdom, the search for a truthful understanding of the human condition, is no longer at the forefront of the minds or activities of many philosophers. For many, philosophy is now concerned with linguistic analysis or perhaps with a survey of the historical landscape of the history of ideas. Yet truth has always been at the centre of human endeavours. Poets, artists and writers have sought truth and devoted their lives to it. Countries have gone to war to defend it and virtuous people have put all else to one side to enter its service. Scientists have been inspired by it and generation after generation of young people have grown up with a conviction that the point of education is to seek truth and to see the world in a more truthful light. The conviction that some forms of behaviour are 'better' — inherently more valuable and more worthwhile — than others underlies all human society, even if agreement on precisely what form this takes is not always easily achieved.

Once truth is abandoned, the distinction between truth and falsity disappears. Witnesses in a court case swear to tell the truth; truth telling is associated with virtue and a denial of truth leads to the collapse of virtue. It has always been a premise of major religions that living truthfully is central to the human enterprise. In fact, one of the features of evil forces is their association with lies.[3] Propaganda aims precisely to undermine the distinction between truth and lies. The idea that there is no distinction would be its greatest achievement and allows those with the loudest media voice to determine and control not just morality but human perceptions of reality itself.

Fundamental human rights as well as duties and obligations become radically undermined once truth is denied. The Nuremberg war crimes trials and similar trials in more recent times are not simply the victors' morality judging the vanquished, as has sometimes been claimed. If they were, then there would be no essential difference between the morality of the SS guards, Pol Pot, Ghandi and Nelson Mandela. War crimes trials are based on the fundamental conviction that certain forms of behaviour are, in an absolute sense, wrong and that there is, in the final analysis, a distinction between right and wrong that must be defended. This conviction transcends any idea of simply defending one's cultural norms against those of another culture.

This book is divided into three parts:

Part 1: In the first part, three ways of underpinning truth and the nature of the debate between realists and anti-realists will be outlined. Anti-realism will be shown to be highly persuasive and its conclusions to have some parallels with those of post-modernism. This chapter will also look at constructivism in psychology and the parallels this has with anti-realism.

Part 2: In the second part, the divide in the philosophic road after Kant will be examined, and the influence of Dostoyevsky through Ivan Karamazov and Nietzsche will be argued to be profound. It will also argue that one path leads to post-modernism, anti-realism and relativity. This is the path that culminates in the perceived views of meaninglessness and in some of the problems our society faces today.

Part 3: The third part will set out an alternative and neglected pathway that lay open after Kant. This will be explored and its development traced through the insights of Kierkegaard and Wittgenstein as well as those of Vaclav Havel and the Hasidic Jewish rabbi, the Kotzker. I will argue that the search for a truthful understanding of the world and the human condition is essential. However, this search also necessarily carries with it an attitude of humility that many religious believers fail to exhibit. I will maintain that many new religious movements and cults, as well as longer established religious groups, are guilty of this failure.

I invite you on a journey, an argument if you like. This book will maintain that those who claim truth in the area of religion and morality by definition may not have it, and that those who do not think they have it may be nearer to it than they know. It will reject the two poles of fundamentalism and relativitism, and it will try to chart a way between these perilous and persuasive rocks.

SETTING OUT THE PROBLEM

There is a moral dimension to the study of truth and knowledge. There have been periods in history when scepticism was rampant, and in these periods a whole way of life and morality was called into question. Once the process of questioning what we know seriously begins, it gives rise to a moral uneasiness. Two examples will illustrate this.

The Greek philosopher Protagoras' claim that 'man is the measure of all things' was a position of scepticism whereby human perception of reality was the final arbiter of certainty. Out of the relativism that this implied arose Plato's writings on moral issues, particularly Plato's *Theatetus* in which he portrays Socrates expressing admiration for the wisdom of Protagoras while not agreeing with him. Socrates and Plato sought to separate knowledge from mere opinion. Knowledge, for Plato, was concerned with the timeless and spaceless Forms which were neither creative nor did they create. The Forms were organised so that the highest Form was the Form of the Good. Knowledge and morality were, therefore, closely related. For Plato, to act badly was due to ignorance, leaving no space for someone knowing what was wrong yet choosing to do this nevertheless.

Descartes sought to provide foundations for knowledge that were absolutely certain, and thus to stem the tide of doubt that prevailed in his time. This was an era when people disagreed about the religious truths which previously had been held as certain. There was, therefore, a moral uneasiness similar to that prevailing before Plato. The Church, as a source for absolute truth claims, came to be substituted, through Luther and other reformers, by the authority of individual conscience and appeal to the Bible. These new and apparent certainties in turn gave way and people no longer knew where they stood.

In both these periods, scepticism was commonly accepted and this was not isolated from a general unease in society. We have the same problem today. There is a general scepticism coupled with a general feeling that Western society has lost its way and has no clear ideas of the values for which it stands or, indeed, if it stands for anything. When Eastern Europe fell to capitalism, it brought supposed benefits such as freedom, but it also brought the lack of values that has become widely accepted in Western society. Freedom in Eastern Europe has been bought at a heavy price, including mass unemployment, lack of food in some areas, the lack of leisure facilities that were generally accepted under the Communist regime, a feeling of hopelessness and a massive increase in corruption. A small elite at the apex of society have prospered hugely, but for the rest the advantages of 'freedom' have been mitigated by many adverse factors. It is not surprising that in parts of Russia and some of the former Soviet satellites there is beginning to be a yearning for the old days with their clearly laid down certainties when at least there was food and employment and the Soviet Union was respected around the world as a superpower. These issues are rarely confronted today since Western interest in values, as in truth, is now peripheral. Yet to many round the world who suffer because of the acceptance of Western 'values' that have been imposed on them, the issues of the ends towards which society is directed are real.

Investigation of knowledge and truth are not self-contained. They affect the whole of society and the way society sees and conducts itself. They affect moral issues from sexuality to business. Understanding the moral uneasiness of society is part of understanding scepticism. This is a preliminary point but one whose significance will emerge later.

Sociologists claim that it is the answers people arrive at which often say more about those seeking the answers than they do about dispassionate inquiry. The motive for asking certain questions often leads to the answers desired by those who ask the question — there is frequently an implicit agenda in place. For instance, in the history of science, the most interesting questions stem from WHY certain sorts of models of understanding are promoted at certain times. For example, the idea of the Earth being the centre of the universe and all stars moving round it fitted perfectly with a religious model which saw the world as one in which God created the first man and woman at the centre of the universe. A picture that allowed human beings to exploit nature in whatever way they wished fitted with a mechanistic universe which arose around the time of Newton. Humans being treated as means rather than as ends in themselves leads to a concentration on a scientific understanding of human nature.

It is often the answers which people seek that determine the questions they ask. This is well illustrated by looking at those who make truth claims for particular interpretations of the Bible:

- Early Christians had no difficulty finding 'the truth' of pacifism abundantly clear in Jesus' teaching. This led to passive resistance to the government and a refusal to fight on behalf of the Roman Empire.
- After Constantine and once the Roman Empire had become Christian, St Augustine soon found 'the truth' that it was legitimate to fight in a just war on behalf of the Christian empire.
- St Thomas Aquinas had no difficult looking to the Bible to justify 'the truth' that God divinely ordained kings to rule and that the structure of society should be feudal with lords, freemen and slaves.
- Wilberforce and his followers appealed to the Bible to justify 'the truth' that slavery was wrong.
- Victorians quoted the Bible to show 'the truth' of women's inferiority to men, and some religious groups still do so.
- Calvinist Africaaners quoted the Bible to help prove 'the truth' that apartheid was permissible.
- Mormons looked to the Bible to justify 'the truth' of their claims about the inferior status of non-Caucasians and women.
- Some Orthodox Jewish writers appeal to the Scriptures to justify 'the truth' of their claim to Jerusalem and the promised land.
- Today militant feminists look to the Bible to establish 'the truth' that Jesus was in favour of the radical equality of male and female.
- By contrast, Conservative Catholics appeal to the Bible to justify 'the truth' of the claim that priests must be male.

The Roman Catholic Church and Protestants of various types have not been shy in claiming truth for their views — indeed a recent document from the Catholic Magisterium was entitled 'Veritatis Splendor'. It is entirely reasonable to hold that truth is splendid and of central importance, but not necessarily that a particular religious group has access to it. The 1998 Catholic encyclical 'ratio et fides' emphasises the importance of the search for truth, but does so from within a faith framework which is held to be immune from challenge. Evangelical Christians of various brands insist that only through Jesus and the word of the Bible can salvation be found and are certain about their rejection of the evils of homosexuality and sex outside marriage.

Today, more than ever, the idea of a search for truth seems to many to be folly. A number of movements have come together which would seem to justify the view that there is no absolute truth and that truth is radically multiple:

- *Post-modernism* rejects any single truth and sees it as being entirely dependent on the viewpoint from which truth is seen.
- In *ethics and aesthetics* what is right and wrong, what is beautiful and ugly is widely accepted as depending on culture and tradition and having no reality independent of such settings. As Hamlet put it, 'There is nothing good or bad but thinking makes it so.'
- In the *philosophy of religion* a growing number of supporters of anti-realism see truth as internal to the language game being played or the story being told. Religious truths, it is held, are not discovered, they are made — religious truths are essentially truths internal to a fictitious story.
- In *mainstream analytic philosophy* there is a general acceptance of the view that the search for any metaphysical underpinning for knowledge is folly. Since the work of Kant and the later Wittgenstein, the search for firm foundations for knowledge or for any metaphysical underpinning has been almost entirely abandoned.

These trends tell us something about the age in which we live — an age in which intellectual scepticism is rampant and the old certainties amount to shibboleths which are regarded as unacceptable and naive. It may well be that the above views are those of a cultural and intellectual elite whose ideas are becoming radically unconnected with the discourse of most 'ordinary' people. Many ordinary people will reject all the above points yet the intellectual elite will affirm them. This disjunction is dangerous for society. One purpose of this book may be to provide the vocabulary to express a deep distrust with, particularly, the above claims. It is infuriating to believe something passionately and to have these views disdained by the elite.

It is important to point out at this stage that relativism is not universal. It is a view of only one group of Western intellectuals and it is too easy to assume that these views are universal. They are not. Another aim of this book is to recognise differences in values between East and West and to hold that there may be ways of resolving these without going down the path of relativism.

The following chapters of this first part look at the way claims to truth are justified by different religious groupings and the claims which sustain the moral values they uphold. It will be argued that all these approaches are fraught with difficulties and that the only sure way of claiming religious truth involves a philosophic position that, while persuasive, many believers will wish to reject.

REALISM AND ANTI-REALISM

First some basic definitions of realism and anti-realism are needed. These, in due course, will need further analysis.

Realism is the theory of truth which claims that a statement is true if it corresponds to the state of affairs that it attempts to describe. Thus:

- 'The cat sat on the mat' is true if, and only if, there is a cat which is sitting on the mat.
- 'This woman is beautiful' is true if and only if this is a woman and she is beautiful. This means being beautiful in some absolute, Platonic sense and not simply because in the culture in which we live this is the accepted view of what constitutes beauty.
- 'An atom is the ultimate indivisible element' is true if, and only if, the ultimate indivisible element is an atom. (We now know, of course that this is false.)
- 'There are green worms on a planet circling Alpha Centurae' is true if, and only if, there are such green worms on the indicated planet. We do not need to know whether such worms exist — for the statement to be true, green worms have to be there.
- 'Murder is wrong' is true if, and only if, murder is in an absolute sense wrong. For this absolute sense to hold true there would need to be some absolute order of value, either one laid down by God

or gods, or to some transcendent order like Plato's Forms which existed timelessly and spacelessly and of which the world around us represents but pale shadows.

Realists affirm bivalence. This means that they maintain that a statement is either true or false depending on whether it does or does not correspond to the state of affairs it sets out to describe. This does not mean that we can necessarily KNOW whether a given statement is either true or false, but this epistemological uncertainty does not undermine the claim that there is a truth to be known. Realists maintain that truth claims are verification transcendent — they do not depend on their ability to be verified.

There are three main categories of realists:

1. *Naive realists* maintain that language is to be taken literally as referring to the object it seeks to describe. For instance, in the religious sphere 'God is angry' or 'God walked in the garden' is held to mean that there is a God and this God really is angry or literally walked in the garden.

2. *Critical realists* such as Janet Martin Soskice maintain that language need not be taken literally but we can refer to states of affairs without describing them literally. For instance, to say that 'Light is a wave' is not literally true; light is not a wave. Nevertheless this is a helpful way of talking about light, and if one uses this phrase one captures something true about the nature of light. In the religious arena, critical realists maintain that it is very difficult to speak literally of God but it is possible to refer to God without describing God, for instance by the use of metaphor. Metaphors such as 'God is my rock' or 'God is my shepherd' are not to be taken literally; nevertheless they refer to God without describing God.

3. *Internal realists* such as Hilary Putnam argue that there may be no single way of referring to a state of affairs, but this does not mean that reference does not take place. There may be various ways in which reference may be made to the same reality and each different way may approximate more or less closely to the reality that is described. However, this does not mean that there is any one successful way of making reference.

All the above are realist positions in that they maintain that the truth of any statement is based on successful reference. They all use a correspondence theory of truth.

Anti-realism, by contrast, rejects correspondence and instead maintains that statements are true because they cohere with other true statements made within a particular form of life.[1] Anti-realists reject all attempts to make language mirror reality, and instead maintain that truth is essentially a human construct. They reject bivalence and instead claim that truth claims are internal to the community in which these truths are expressed. Truth depends on what is agreed within the community which depends on the rules of the language game, not on dispassionate inquiry. In the case of morality, an example would be that within Islam it is true that a man may have four wives but in Western society it is true that only one wife is allowed. Both truths are internal to their respective frameworks.

An example used by Aristotle can help to illustrate the difference between realism and anti-realism about the future. If someone says 'There will be a sea battle tomorrow' then:

The realist about the future will maintain that either this statement is true or it is false. We may not know whether it is true or false, but it is either the one or the other because the statement corresponds to whatever will be the state of affairs tomorrow.

By contrast, *the anti-realist* will say that there is no truth to be known because until tomorrow has come and either a sea battle has been fought or none has occurred, the statement cannot be either true or false. It simply has no truth value at all.

Another example might be taken from the field of literature. Assume someone says 'Mozart produces better music than the Beatles', then:

The realist about music will maintain that there is some absolute standard of music against which the two types of music can be measured, while

The anti-realist will say that within one culture Mozart's music might be more highly rated than that of the Beatles, but there is no absolute standard and in another culture a contrary view might be held.

With this basic initial introduction, the application of these two theories to moral and religious beliefs can be now considered.

Realism and anti-realism are two theories of truth. Realism involves a claim to reference or correspondence, which can be justified in two alternative ways within the fields of morality or religion. These are Natural Theology and Reformed Epistemology, which will be examined in turn. Anti-realism then provides an alternative approach.

NATURAL THEOLOGY

Natural Theology holds to a realist understanding of truth, maintaining that the statement 'God exists' is true because it corresponds to the existence of the God who created and sustains the universe. There are foundations for religious belief and, indeed, for the whole rich 'form of life' of the religious believer which includes prayer, worship, liturgy, morality, and so on. These foundations can be shown to be true through the use of reason.

Natural Theology is the basis for the traditional Roman Catholic approach to understanding religious truth claims. It derives from St Thomas Aquinas and his use of Aristotle's philosophy to provide an intellectual basis for the Christian tradition. It was affirmed by the Council of Trent and more specifically by the First Vatican Council in 1870. Natural Theology maintains that it is possible to arrive at the truth of the claim that 'God exists' as well as certain basic knowledge about God's attributes (for instance, that God is omnipotent, omniscient, wholly simple, immutable, bodiless, timeless and spaceless) by the use of human reason alone. God plays fair with human beings and makes belief in God possible by the use of human reason.

Revealed Theology goes further than Natural Theology and makes accessible to human beings revealed truths which are not accessible to reason. Nothing within Revealed Theology contradicts Natural Theology, however. Thus, many moral commandments such as the Ten Commandments or the prohibitions against adultery can, according to St Thomas Aquinas, be derived from the use of reason alone, but they are also confirmed by revelation. Other revealed doctrines, such as the Christian idea of the Trinity or the creation of the universe, cannot be known by reason but do not go against reason. There is, then, for Aquinas and the Catholic tradition, no tension between reason and revelation.

Natural Theology enables the claim to be made that the statement 'God exists' is true because this claim successfully refers to the God who creates and sustains the universe. It therefore underpins a correspondence theory of truth. The only problem is that attempts to prove the existence of God have failed, as generally agreed today. Various attempts have been made, but without success. Here six of these arguments will be briefly outlined:

1. the cosmological argument
2. the ontological argument
3. the design argument
4. the moral argument
5. the religious experience argument
6. the cumulative case argument.

THE COSMOLOGICAL ARGUMENT

In one of its many forms,[2] the cosmological argument seeks to show that the universe is contingent and dependent on a God who necessarily exists and who is not dependent on anything else. However, this argument depends on many assumptions that cannot be justified, including:

• Leibniz's Principle of Sufficient Reason which rejects the idea of an infinite regress of causes. This claims that there must be a complete or total explanation for everything and this demands a first cause. However, there seems to be no compelling reason why there must be a complete explanation; perhaps any explanation will only ever be partial.

• the idea that uncaused causes are impossible. It is held that the universe could not have come into existence from nothing as 'nothing can come from nothing'. This has already been challenged at the micro-particle level by some scientists who maintain that particles can come into existence from nothing.

• the claim that the idea of a necessarily existent substance is a possible idea. To say that God is a 'necessarily existent substance' is to use terminology which avoids referring to God as a being or a thing. God is not a being among other beings nor is God a thing like an undiscovered planet. However, God necessarily exists independent of the universe God has created and sustains. Hume and Kant, however, rejected the whole idea of God as being 'necessarily existent'. They maintained that anything that exists may or may not exist and the idea of necessity only applies to linguistic convention. For instance, 'All spinsters are female' may be held to be necessarily true because of the way we use words.

• that the necessarily existent, wholly simple, timeless and spaceless substance at which the cosmological argument attempts to arrive is the same as the personal God of Christianity. Aquinas names the unmoved mover, the uncaused cause at which his arguments arrive as 'God', but this timeless, spaceless, bodiless, immutable 'something' seems to many a long way from the personal, loving God of much of the Christian tradition.

None of the above assumptions are easily sustainable and all are questionable. The cosmological argument as a pointer to the existence of God is therefore, at most, of limited value.

The cosmological argument also rejects the claim that the universe is an explicable brute fact,[3] and it maintains that to postulate a God is a simpler explanation for the universe than the claim that the universe is inexplicable. Both these positions are, also, highly debatable.

THE ONTOLOGICAL ARGUMENT

The ontological argument seeks to move from:

a definition of God — that the statement 'God exists' is *de dicto* necessarily true (*de dicto* meaning that the necessity rests on the way words are used) — to

the reality of God — that the statement 'God exists' is *de re* necessarily true (*de re* meaning that the necessity of God's existence resides in the very nature of the substance that is God, in that God does not depend on anything else for God's existence and did not come into and cannot go out of existence).

Aquinas rejected the ontological argument. He maintained that human beings could not know God's essence and could not, therefore, know whether God's essence included existence. Aquinas also thought that there was no agreement on a definition of God — after all some religious people think that God has a body and Aquinas thought that this was absurd.

Both Hume and Kant showed that it is not possible to move from the *de dicto* necessity of a proposition to the *de re* necessity of God. In other words, one cannot move from the idea of God to the reality of God. They also challenged the very idea of anything being 'necessary', maintaining that the only things that are necessary are linguistic statements where truth represents convention (for instance *de dicto* necessary statements such as 'All triangles have three angles').

The most that the ontological argument can show is that, within a religious form of life, the statement 'God necessarily exists' is true. The nature of this truth claim is one that I shall explore in due course and has much more to do with an anti-realist understanding of truth than with a realist claim.[4]

THE DESIGN ARGUMENT

This argument depends on key assumptions, in particular that the order in the universe is the result of design rather than chance. The existence of order in the universe is undoubted, but this does not mean that the universe is designed and, of course, design implies a designer. The design argument seeks to establish that the needs of human beings and animals have been anticipated and planned for by an intelligence named God or that the whole mechanism of evolution was put in place by God in order to bring about God's purpose. However, the design argument is unable to refute the contrary position that human beings and animals evolved to fit the conditions that are available and, in other conditions, different organisms would have evolved. Darwin's theory of natural selection was a major challenge to religion in the nineteenth century as it provided a mechanism which explains evolution and there is no apparent need for God to have created human beings directly or indirectly.

The design argument also has difficulty explaining the existence of natural evil or of an evolutionary system that is cruel in the extreme and involves every species preying on other species in a manner which, to a disinterested observer, must appear morally unacceptable. The argument is also susceptible to John Mill's challenge that, even if it succeeded, the God it pointed to would be limited since any being who had to use means (such as evolution) to bring about the chosen ends could not bring these ends directly. Mill therefore concluded that the most that the design argument could achieve was to postulate a designer who might be benevolent but was severely limited in power. Even this conclusion, however, is one that few non-theistic philosophers would accept.

THE MORAL ARGUMENT

Moral arguments either:

- start from assumptions about the existence of an absolute moral order and then attempt to postulate a mind which is held to be the source of these moral rules, or
- seek to work from the existence of conscience implanted in human beings by God or gods as this faculty could not, so it is claimed, have evolved.[5]

Again, neither of these claims can be established and the hypothesis that moral codes are a product of human society or are grounded in our common humanity is not easily refuted.

THE RELIGIOUS EXPERIENCE ARGUMENT

These arguments seek to move from claimed experiences of God, some mysterious presence or power, to the reality of God, or the existence of the power that would explain the experience. However, there is an unbridgeable gulf between:

'It appeared to me that God, the Virgin Mary, Kali or a mysterious power appeared to me last night',
and
'God, the Virgin Mary, Kali or a mysterious power appeared to me last night'.

The fact that one is certain of something does not make the claim true. To those who already believe in God, Mary, Kali or some mysterious power, apparent experiences of these substances or entities may help to confirm their existing belief, but such experiences cannot establish the existence of God to those with no prior belief. At most, an individual who has such experiences may be convinced, but there is no reason why others should be persuaded unless the prior probability of God's existence can first be established.[6]

In a way there are parallels with claimed experiences of UFOs. Large numbers of people in the United States believe in the existence of UFOs and aliens, but this does not mean that others should accept the reports. What is more, experiences are often deceptive, hence experience cannot be the bedrock of certainty as John Locke and the empiricists claimed.

Effectively, the claim to a religious experience depends on an individual's assessment of the prior probability of the existence of that which it is claimed is being experienced. This prior probability cannot be established to the satisfaction of a rational and independent observer, and without this prior probability, the argument from religious experience of God fails. This argument is linked to the next one.

THE CUMULATIVE CASE ARGUMENT

Basil Mitchell[7] and, subsequently, Richard Swinburne,[8] have put forward probability and cumulative case arguments for the existence of God. They maintain that the existence of God is, on balance, more probable than not. Both hold that it is not possible to prove the existence of God, but putting together a wide body of evidence may make it more likely than not that God exists. Much, however, depends on which factors are taken as evidence. For instance, the presence of beauty, order and the yearnings of human beings for a sense of ultimate purpose may point to the existence of God. On the other hand, the presence of evil, suffering, natural disasters, diseases and the ability of scientific laws to explain an increasing part of the universe may render the existence of God less likely.

The assessment of probability is always a highly subjective judgment, and what one person considers to be probable, another may consider unlikely. Nevertheless, this approach does have some merit, although it also has limitations. I will return to it in due course.

None of the above arguments are convincing in establishing the existence of God as traditionally defined. The most that they may achieve is to point to some very vague transcendence lying beyond all the main religious systems. This would be so vague, however, that it could not serve as a basis to underwrite any one of the systems. It is popular today to claim that 'All religions are the same really' or that all world religions point to a single, underlying reality. It is a nice idea, but the evidence for it is limited and tends to owe more to the wish for this to be the case by some commentators and experts in 'religious studies' than to dispassionate assessment of the argument or evidence.

The three great monotheistic religions, Christianity, Islam and Judaism, all believe in a single God. Christians believe that God is Trinitarian and that Jesus was God's son, and Islam heavily emphasises the oneness of God and sees Jesus as a prophet sent by God but no more than this. There seems to be little agreement about what the word 'God' refers to, however. Within Christianity, for example, traditional Catholic theology maintains that God is wholly simple, timeless, spaceless, immutable and bodiless. By contrast, Protestants, as well as Liberation and Process theologians, consider God to be in time and suffering with humanity. These conceptions are not easily reconciled.[9] Hinduism affirms many gods, although there may be a single underlying reality beyond these different manifestations. In some strands Buddhism rejects any idea of God, while in other strands some limited idea of a deity may be present. Any claim that there is a single underlying reality beyond all religions tends to do violence to the beliefs of all the main traditions and to take out of them all that they consider to be distinctive and possibly essential.

Assuming that the above summary of the arguments to prove the existence of God is fair, then the basis for the claim to reference established by the use of reason fails. Two conclusions can be drawn:

1. The most that reason may establish is the possibility or, conceivably, the probability of the existence of God, but it provides no details about this God.
2. For those who have religious faith, the faith tends to be unconditional and the centre of their life. To hold that God's existence is merely possible may not do justice to the 'all or nothing' commitment which religious faith involves.

Another means of establishing a basis for realist religious truth claims, therefore, needs to be found — that is, for the claim that 'God exists' is true (if, indeed, it is true) because this refers to the God who created and sustains the universe. In recent years one such method has come from philosophers in the United States, called Reformed Epistemologists.

REFORMED EPISTEMOLOGY

This approach uses a realist understanding of truth. The statement 'God exists' is held to be true because it corresponds to the existence of the being, substance or spirit named God who or which created and sustains the universe. There are, it is claimed, foundations for religious belief and, indeed, for the whole rich 'form of life' of the religious believer which includes prayer, worship, liturgy, morality, and so on. These foundations can be shown to be true through the use of revelation.

Reformed Epistemologists belong to the Protestant reformed tradition, and see their theology as being rooted in the approach of Calvin or Luther and, prior to this, in Augustine and Anselm. They totally reject the approach taken by Natural Theology. Indeed, Karl Barth maintained that of all the reasons for rejecting Catholicism, Natural Theology was the greatest.

The reformed tradition rejects the supremacy of reason as human reason is fallen[10] and is unable to understand the nature of God, let alone arrive at the existence of God. To assert the priority of reason is arrogant and presumptuous. Reformed Epistemology claims the believer can hold to the truth of the foundations of belief without justification.

Both supporters of Natural Theology and of Reformed Epistemology agree that there are foundations for knowledge and that these foundations are true because they correspond. Where Reformed Epistemologists differ from supporters of Natural Theology is that they reject reliance on human reason. To them it makes no sense to doubt that God exists and, because of this, they hold to the 'proper basicality' of belief in God as one of the foundations for their whole way of looking at the world.

The basis for the Reformed Epistemologists' claim is that their noetic structure (the whole structure of their knowing and the way they look at the world) is correctly ordered, while those who deny the existence of God have a defective noetic structure. The latter fail to see the world correctly. Christian Reformed Epistemologists claim that they do not simply know the truth but that their way of seeing the world is the correct way of seeing the world because God has given them grace to be able to see the world as it really is through God's revelation. Those who do not share their view are held not to have received God's grace, and to be the victims of their own pride and arrogance in presuming to assert that reason can judge God. The doctrine of the Fall and of Adam and Eve's disobedience is often brought in to support their position. This is used to buttress the claim that, due to the Fall and to human sinfulness, human nature and with it human reason is incapable of seeing the world correctly through it's own unaided power, hence the need for God's grace.

The reason that some people receive God's grace and others do not varies. The main alternatives are:

1. God predestines some people for salvation and some for damnation. Grace cannot be earned and can only be accepted. It is God's free choice to save some and not others, and God's decision can only be accepted. This position makes the choice of who will be saved arbitrary and something that the human individual cannot influence. It also seems radically unfair, although it may be argued, as St Thomas Aquinas did, that since God is our 'owner' and 'creator', he has total rights over us and we have no right to question God — a position many modern writers question.

2. God makes grace available to everyone but each person has to decide whether to accept this. If this position is held, grace becomes largely irrelevant except to provide some assistance once a decision for faith has been taken, because it is the free decision of the individual which will determine whether grace is received and not some choice by God.

3. God awards grace to the virtuous and withholds it from those who do evil. On this basis, grace is again largely irrelevant as those who are virtuous are saved and those who are not are condemned. It also makes it difficult to explain virtuous people who are not, for instance, Christians since if the virtuous receive grace and therefore faith one would expect all those who are virtuous to have faith — which is clearly not the case.

4. God gives grace to all those who believe as they ought to believe. This becomes a circular argument because the Reformed Epistemologists are claiming that 'believing correctly' is due to God's grace and if grace depends on believing correctly an absurd situation arises.

Reformed Epistemologists will not try to convert those who disagree with them by rational argument as this would be to fall into the trap of those who reject revelation. Instead they may preach at the non-believer or pray for them and attempt thereby to bring them to accept the truth of revelation and, thereby, to be able to see the world correctly.

To the Christian Reformed Epistemologist God's presence in speaking to him or her is so direct and immediate that no further form of justification for their belief is needed or called for. This can happen in two ways:

1. The Reformed Epistemologist considers that God 'speaks' through the Bible — not just in the sense that the Bible is 'inspired' by God, but also because God speaks to the individual reader in each generation as he or she reads the Bible for themselves. There are two primarily Protestant presuppositions here (and, of course, Reformed Epistemology comes from Protestantism, having its origins in the theology of Calvin):

   a) A high value is accorded to the accuracy of the Biblical text. In support of this it might be argued that the Gospels were written or compiled from existing material between thirty and seventy years after the death of Jesus, and some of the epistles were written after an even shorter period. The Magdalen Papyrus, which was given to Magdalen College at Oxford by Charles Huleatt in 1901, was dated by Carsten Peter Thiede to within forty years of Jesus' death. This reinforced the view that much of the Gospel material is based on accounts written or dictated by those who were present with Jesus, thereby increasing the reliability of the stories.[11]

   b) God is held to speak directly to the individual when he or she reads the Bible. Revelation did not, therefore, take place only during Jesus' life, but continues when the individual reads the Bible in the right spirit. A person is, therefore, considered to be in the presence of God when they read and God is held to speak to the reader directly through the text.

2. The Reformed Epistemologist considers that there is no need to justify or intellectually validate the framework or foundations of his or her belief as the individual is directly aware of the presence of God. It is as if I am directly aware of the presence of my closest friends. I do not need to seek validation for their presence as their presence is so clear and obvious to me that talk of verifying this seems out of place. So it may be with the Christian's awareness of God. To demand rational support for the existence of God is, to

the believer, as ridiculous, so it is claimed, as to demand rational support for my awareness of my friends.

The Reformed Epistemologists effectively construct an argument which maintains that they have the Truth (on a realist understanding) and that this is so obvious that it needs no justification. God's grace and revelation guarantee the world being seen rightly.

The reply to this position is obvious. Many religious groups around the world could maintain exactly the same thing with equal passion and conviction. Sadly, however, passion and conviction are no guarantee of truth. In fact in too many cases in the past religious certainties have been the cause of evil and wicked actions.[12] Modern religious people would almost universally condemn these actions, yet those who perpetrated such actions did so in the conviction that they were right.

Muslims students at my College at the University of London sometimes approach me with incredulity that I cannot see the 'obvious' truth of Islam. To them, Islam is so clearly true and the revelation in the Holy Koran to the prophet Mohammed is so obvious that it seems incredible that any open-minded person who seeks truth could fail to see this truth. Evangelical Christians at New College, University of New South Wales in Sydney had exactly the same reaction when I delivered the lectures on which this book is based. It was significant that a minority of Christian students at New College found the approach I outlined liberating despite the heavy peer pressure from the evangelical majority at New College. The same position will be taken by supporters of other religious truth claims throughout the world and it shows the problem that Reformed Epistemology faces. If there are no rational criteria to judge between competing truth claims, the idea of any basis for particular realist claims seems to be seriously undermined.

Neither Natural Theology, therefore, nor Reformed Epistemology seems able to underwrite the claim to truth in a realist sense. This opens the way for a third approach, which rejects the realism position entirely.

ANTI-REALISM

Anti-realism holds a different view of truth but still maintains that the statement 'God exists' is true. This truth is accepted and endorsed by the rich Christian, Islamic and Judaic traditions. Similar claims are made by the other great world religions in which these claims are similarly central to their belief structures. There are foundations for religious belief and, indeed, for the whole rich 'form of life' of the religious believer which includes prayer, worship, liturgy, morality, and so on. The anti-realist will also agree with the Reformed Epistemologist in rejecting the claim of Natural Theology to be able to prove the existence of God, on the basis that none of the arguments for the existence of God succeed. They will further agree that the existence of God is obvious to the believer and does not need rational support. Indeed, that it is a characteristic of belief that it is not tentative and does not depend on probability.

Where anti-realists will disagree with both Natural Theology and Reformed Epistemology is that the anti-realists reject the whole idea of truth being based on correspondence. Statements are held to be true because they are held to be true and accepted within a given form of life.

Within any given form of religious life, certain statements are held to be true, for instance:

• Within Islam, the statements 'There is one God who is Allah and Mohammed is his prophet' and 'The Holy Koran was dictated by Allah to Mohammed' are unquestionably true.
• Within Judaism, it is unquestionably true that God is the father of the Jewish nation and God promised the land of Israel (however defined) to Abraham and to Abraham's descendants through Isaac (which means to the Jews) in perpetuity.
• Within Roman Catholicism, the statement 'The Pope, when speaking *ex cathedra*, can promulgate dogmas which, once they have been received by the Church, must be accepted by the faithful' is true.
• Within evangelical Christianity, the statement 'God has redeemed us through Christ Jesus who has died for our sins and has revealed God to us through the pages of Holy Scripture' is accepted without question.

None of these statements can be verified by evidence which would convince neutral observers. To be sure, they seem more or less to be confirmed by the stories held fast by certain traditions, but these stories have been passed down by an oral tradition over longer or shorter periods of time. One set of stories is, inherently, no more likely than another, at least to a disinterested outside observer. Those within each group will, naturally, consider their own stories to be far more probable than any others. Each group of believers will strongly maintain that their stories and claims are true because they can be independently verified, but none of them will accept the verifications proposed by other religious groups except in so far as they accord with their own.

Jews look to Abraham as the father of the Jewish nation and regard this nation as the inheritor of God's promise to Abraham. Muslims look to Abraham as the father of the Arab nation and see themselves as inheritors of God's promise through Ishmael. Christians look to Abraham as the 'father of faith'. Meanwhile some Biblical scholars point out that the figure of Abraham probably never even existed. Abraham may well be a mythical figure based on oral stories handed down and built on over hundreds of years. There is not the slightest evidence outside the Biblical stories that there was such a man as Abraham and the only 'evidence' is that contained within the stories accepted within the different religious traditions.

The anti-realist maintains that the whole idea of a search for evidence is out of place. Religious truths are not subject to proof — in this they agree with the Reformed Epistemologists. People are educated into a form of life. As the Hegelian philosopher Bradley said, individuals are not born into a desert, they are inculcated into a tradition. Wittgenstein rejected the whole idea of language having foundations that can be proved in the way that both Catholic Natural Theology and Reformed Epistemology assume. Instead, people are educated into a form of life which takes for granted a certain way of looking at the world. Doubting and questioning our different forms of life are sophisticated activities which only take place at a late stage of development — perhaps when we have learnt to be philosophers. Underpinning all our forms of life is a general 'agreement in judgment' which it does not make sense to doubt.

It may be worth unpacking this position in more detail as it is crucial to understanding the origins of the anti-realist view. The philosophic underpinnings of the anti-realist position are of considerable interest, and are outlined in the next chapter. However, if you wish you can skip chapter 3 and move directly to p. 38.

SUMMARY

There are two basic theories of truth:

1. *Realism* holds that statements are true because they correspond or refer. Thus moral and religious statements would be true if and only if these correspond or refer to a God who creates and sustains the universe, or to some absolute order of morality. However, neither reason (Natural Theology) nor revelation (Reformed Epistemology) provide any adequate basis for realist claims to truth. The passion and conviction of those who hold such truth claims is no guarantee of their validity.

2. *Anti-realism* maintains that statements are true because they cohere with other statements that are accepted as true within a given form of life. Thus specific religious and moral claims will be true in the societies where these claims are accepted. There is no absolute truth — Christian, Hindu, Islamic, Jewish and Sikh truths are all true for the religious believers who assent to these systems of thought.

In the absence of any adequate and generally accepted grounds for realist truth claims in morality, religion, aesthetics or other fields, it would appear that anti-realism is the most persuasive and rational course to follow. It allows truth claims to be accepted but sees these claims as being dependent on the system within which they are made.

3

FOUNDATIONS WITHOUT INDUBITABILITY

THE LEGACY FROM RENE DESCARTES AND JOHN LOCKE

For nearly two thousand years philosophers have sought foundations for knowledge, some secure bedrock on which all our claims to know can be built. It was, however, Rene Descartes who took this approach to the extreme point. He resolved to try to doubt everything in order to arrive at something indubitable, some sure place that could provide the bedrock for certainty.

For Descartes, the greatest certainty was found by retreating inside one's mind, by doubting everything to arrive at clear and distinct ideas. He puts his case like this:

> I resolved to assume that everything that ever entered into my mind was no more true than the illusions of my dreams. But immediately afterwards I noticed that while I thus wished to think all things false, it was absolutely essential that the 'I' who thought this should be somewhat, and remarking that this truth I think therefore I am was so certain and assured that all the most extravagant suppositions brought forward by the sceptics were incapable of shaking it, I came to the conclusion that I could receive it without scruple as the first principle of the Philosophy for which I was seeking.[1]

Descartes' 'first principle' was the Cogito (*Cogito Ergo Sum*, I think therefore I am). Because he could think, he could not deny that he was a thinking thing. However, this alone was not enough to underwrite claims to knowledge. Descartes needed a further step.

Descartes considered that he could not conceive God as not existing; existence was part of the very idea of God. God was clearly and distinctly seen by him to exist, and as God's existence was inseparable from the idea of God, just as three angles were inseparable from the idea of a triangle, so God must, indeed, exist. Therefore, Descartes thought, once he had established that:

1. he existed, and
2. God existed,

he could then go on to claim to know many more things because God could be brought in to guarantee that any 'clear and distinct' ideas Descartes had were, in fact, correct. The only problem — in fact, one of the major problems — is that Descartes effectively put forward a form of the ontological argument for God's existence, and this does not work. He claimed that because we have a clear idea of God and that this idea includes God's existence, there must be a God in reality. However, Kant and Hume clearly showed that it is impossible to move from an idea to reality — whatever an idea may contain, it shows us nothing about the way reality actually is. I may well know that there cannot be a unicorn without it having a horn, but that does not mean that there are any unicorns or any horns! Similarly, IF God exists, then God may indeed have to exist in a sense that is not dependent on anything else. The problem is, however, the little word 'if' and one cannot dispense with this just because one has a clear idea. Without God to guarantee that Descartes' clear and distinct ideas correspond to reality, his epistemological system for underwriting claims to knowledge fails.

John Locke took a different but related approach. He, too, sought certainty and a foundation for knowledge claims, but he found this certainty in experience. Locke, like Descartes, believed in God and considered that there was a divide between what could be known by reason and what could be known by revelation. However, he faced the problem of how revelation was to be verified, and to do this he appealed to experience, specifically to the claims of miracles. Thus he wrote:

Moses saw the burning bush without it being consumed and heard a voice out of it. This was something besides finding an impulse upon his mind to go to Pharoah, that he might bring his brethren out of Egypt: and yet he thought not this enough to authorise him to go without that message, till God, by another miracle of his rod turned into a serpent, had assured him of a power to testify his mission, by the same miracle repeated before them, whom he was sent to. Gideon was sent by an angel to deliver Israel from the Midianites, and yet he desired a sign to convince him that his commission was from God. These, and several like instances to be found among the prophets of old, are enough to show that they thought not an inward seeing of persuasion in their own minds, without any other proof, a sufficient evidence that it was from God.[2]

Locke claims that experience underlies all knowledge but, of course, experience can be false. It appears to us that the sun goes round the Earth but it does not. It appears to us that a stick in water is bent, but it is not. It appears that there is an oasis in the desert, but it is a mirage. What is more, that which is experienced depends heavily on prior presuppositions and our cultural background. Experience is not 'innocent'; we bring to our experiences many presuppositions and 'ways of seeing' that determine what we see and experience. We cannot, therefore, guarantee certainty. What is more, to appeal to miracles to verify revelation fails as the evidence for miracles is highly disputed. Even more disputed is what, if anything, they verify. Extraordinary events may, indeed, occur, but the appropriate response to an inexplicable event may be to seek explanation by undertaking scientific research rather than to appeal to 'God' as an explanation.

These two approaches to foundations for knowledge, ideas and experience have underpinned all attempts to justify knowledge up until the beginning of this century, and the work of G.E. Moore.

G.E. MOORE: *IN DEFENCE OF COMMON SENSE*

G.E. Moore's *In Defence of Common Sense* was a turning point in that he rejected the idea that there were indubitable foundations for knowledge. Most philosophers recognise his article as being of major importance but there is disagreement about what its exact importance is. G.E. Moore attempted to undercut the philosophic search for indubitable foundations by appealing to common sense. He claimed that there were certain banal statements that it simply did not make sense to doubt and these statements were basic. They included statements such as the following:

- 'I have never been to the moon.'
- 'There is a living body that is my body.'
- 'This is a hand.'
- 'That is a radiator.'

Statements such as these simply cannot be doubted — at least in our form of life. Of course, a caveman would not know what a radiator was, but to us that the thing on the wall is a radiator is an unquestioned part of the form of life into which we have been educated. The Scottish philosopher David Hume made something of the same point when, after doing some intensive philosophy, he said:

> The intense view of these manifold imperfections in human reason has so wrought upon me and heated my brain, that I am ready to reject all belief and reasoning and can look on no opinion as more probable or likely than any other ...

> I dine, I play a game of backgammon, I converse and am merry with my friends and when after three or four hours amusement I would return to these speculations, they appear so cold and strained and ridiculous that I cannot find it in my heart to enter into them any further.[3]

Only an academic philosopher, and then only while doing philosophy, could doubt Moore's propositions. Anyone who seriously doubts that 'This is a hand' is not a candidate for philosophic discussion but for the madhouse. The power of Moore's propositions lies in the fact that you cannot find anyone who could deny them other than in academic discussion.

Moore said that his propositions are much more certain than anything from which they could possibly be derived. If anyone wanted to assert the opposite of these basic propositions, he would be at a loss to grasp what they meant. What is characteristic of Moore's propositions is that disagreement about them is so very difficult. In 'In Defence of Common Sense' he brings to our attention the large number of expressions about which no justification in the form of a supporting belief is required.

Moore's propositions rest not only on agreement but on his view that they are true. For Moore, what we agree about is as important as our agreement. So his view is not that truth is guaranteed by agreement but that you can only press for justification in cases where it makes sense to do so, and, in the case of Moore's examples, it does not. It is senseless to push further back as the regress of justification has nowhere else to go. This is crucial in understanding the challenge of anti-realism.

Quinton in *The Nature of Things* argues that there are logically intuitive beliefs which are the foundation of all our knowledge claims. Although Moore's propositions have all the characteristic of logically intuitive beliefs, they are so banal as not to be capable of being the foundation for any edifice of knowledge. It is because of their ordinariness that we cannot understand anyone doubting them. It seems absurd that a philosopher should hold up his hand and say, 'this is a hand', and that this insight should transform philosophy. Yet, that is what happened with Moore's paper. Moore showed that there are statements which it does not make sense to doubt, and this is now widely accepted. What Moore did not do, however, was to work out the precise role these statements had. For Moore, these statements provided the foundation for knowledge claims just as Descartes thought that the foundation lay in ideas and Locke considered the foundation to lie in experience. It took the work of the later Wittgenstein to recognise the importance of Moore's statements and why Moore was mistaken in his claims about the role they played.

WITTGENSTEIN AND *ON CERTAINTY*

Wittgenstein is probably the most influential philosopher of the twentieth century. His early work, *Tractatus Logico-Positivus* had the same objectives as his later work: to clear up problems that had puzzled philosophers, not by solving them but by dissolving them and showing that when these puzzles were correctly understood they ceased to be puzzles at all. Wittgenstein wished to bring philosophers peace by dissolving the conundrums that perplexed them. His way of doing this changed from his early to his later work, but his objectives were the same.

The preface to Wittgenstein's *On Certainty*[4] described the work as a discussion of Moore's claims in *In Defence of Common Sense*. Wittgenstein was not, however, interested in common sense. Rather, he was concerned with the peculiar logical role played by the statements Moore had identified. Wittgenstein's claim was that Moore was right to say that the propositions he identified were indubitable, but he was mistaken to say that they were true: 'Moore has every right to say that there is a tree in front of him. Naturally he may be wrong.' What Moore was really trying to do was to 'Enumerate a lot of empirical claims which we affirm without special testing and which have a peculiar logical role'.[5]

In spite of the indubitability of Moore's propositions such as 'This is a hand' and 'There is a human body which is my human body', there is something inappropriate about the claim to know them. Moore says that we can know them with certainty, but the word 'know' seems to fit uncomfortably with such banal propositions as 'This is a hand'.

Wittgenstein made clear that the idea of a private language simply does not make sense. We learn a language and with it a form of life — we grow up not as isolated individuals, but in a rich world of experience which we share with others. We are educated into this world from our earliest days and early childhood is essentially about coming to terms with this world. In so doing, we learn the conventions of language and therefore are able to communicate. For example, a child learns the meaning of words such as chair, table and dad at between one and two years of age. You do not find a two-year-old saying 'Are you really my dad?'. Doubting that the person you think is your dad is really your dad is a later development — doubt about initial assumptions is a higher level activity.[6] It is only a philosopher, and then while doing philosophy, who would doubt that the object in front of them is a table. For the rest of us, we are educated into a form of life in which various statements are taken for granted. They represent the bedrock of all our knowledge claims. Similarly, to say 'I know' is subsequent to learning the grounds of our form of life. It is a mistake to think we know these grounds, the bedrock. Rather, they are the unquestioned ground rules of all that we do.

Wittgenstein said that when we reach bedrock, our spade is turned and we have to say 'this is simply what we do'. His point is that justification comes to an end and the ground rules of the form of life are not dubitable or provable. This is, of course, a rejection of a way of thinking in philosophy that had persisted for two-and-a-half thousand years. It is to reject epistemology (the study of knowledge) altogether and with it any idea of indubitable foundations. Instead of seeking an unattainable metaphysical certainty, the philosopher's task becomes that of seeking to understand how language works. Wittgenstein differs from Moore in that Moore holds that the bedrock statements that underpin our forms of life are true, whereas Wittgenstein claims that it does not make sense to doubt them. The two positions are subtly but importantly different.

There have been various interpretations of Wittgenstein's argument against private language, but the main thrust of his position is clear. A person does not have an interior feeling which is unnamed and inexplicable, and then attempts to attach a label to it, which he may (or may not) call 'pain'. This idea of retreating into one's own mind to arrive at certainty is a legacy of Descartes and was considered by Wittgenstein as being profoundly misguided. A person does not remember this first sensation and when he comes across another inner sensation rather similar to the first, decide to attach the same label to the second experience. How would he, in any case, decide whether to attach the word 'pain' to what might otherwise be called an 'ache', a 'laugh' or a 'pang of hunger'? If language were private, then what one attached words to would be arbitrary. Words are not given meaning by inner concentration. Rather, they have a meaning which is agreed on within a given community. The child learns these words and what they represent. The child learns the rules of language and it is only because language does have rules that communication between individuals is possible at all.

There is 'agreement in judgment' within a community and it is only because there is such basic agreement that disagreement is possible. It is only because we are educated into a form of life where there is agreed meaning for words such as chair, table, air conditioner, light bulb, human being, and so on, that we can argue and differ about less basic matters. Indeed one reason that philosophers are so often seen by non-philosophers as being foolish and irrelevant is that they ask questions about state of affairs which every normal person (except for children who have not yet been fixed into a particular way of looking at the world) take for granted.

The strength of Wittgenstein's passages on privacy in the *Investigations* is that they make talk of knowledge as a private, internal thing really impossible. The general point made by Wittgenstein is the same as that lying behind Plato's arguments in the *Theatetus* (particularly his 'aviary' argument (198) which is meant to reduce the private conception of rightness and sureness to absurdity). If truth and rightness have an internal criterion of truth, then it is difficult to see how we can ever make mistakes. Wittgenstein's private language arguments are of great significance not so much because of his rejection of the idea of a private language (which is generally accepted) as in his rejection of the idea of people retreating into their shell and looking out. This is a common view for philosophers to take, and philosophers of religion are particularly vulnerable to it. The temptation to 'look inside oneself' is very strong but, as Wittgenstein put it: 'You won't find out about sensation by watching yourself when you've got a headache.'

Wittgenstein's anti-private language argument needs to be seen in conjunction with his treatment of Moore's banal propositions. We are educated into a form of life, and Moore's propositions are part of the grounds rules for our form of life. As Wittgenstein said:

> If language is to be a means of communication there must be agreement not only in definitions but also (queer as this may sound) in judgments. This seems to abolish logic but does not do so.[7]

Wittgenstein was saying that in order for us to have disagreements, in order for us to argue, we first have to agree about things. There has to be prior agreement not reached by reasoning. We are educated into a form of life at our parents' knees and we learn the ground rules of a form of life. We learn what a table, a chair, a bookcase and a hand are. These are not proved to us, rather they are the unquestioned ground rules for the form of life we inhabit. They are held fast by all that surrounds them and they are, indeed, indubitable. We cannot doubt them until we are old enough to become philosophers, and even then doubt is very difficult.

Wittgenstein said that it is difficult to realise the groundlessness of our form of life. He rejected the idea of there being any indubitable foundations because at the end of justification there are grounds that cannot themselves be justified. There are foundations, but they are foundations because they are unquestioned within a particular form of life, not because of their indubitable nature. As Wittgenstein said: 'A child must learn the use of colour before it can ask the name of a colour.' The ground rules of our form of life are a given — they are unquestioned assumptions within the form of life we inhabit — but Moore's mistake was to claim truth for these grounds. Certain grounds are held unshakeably fast by what surrounds them. This is why religious believers, for instance, regard blasphemy as so threatening because it challenges a whole structure of belief.

Within any society, there is agreement in judgment on the ground rules of the form of life shared by that society. Language is, therefore, based on following rules[8] and Moore's propositions are fundamental ground rules of our form of life. We cannot justify the ground rules. Thus Wittgenstein wrote:

> 'How am I to obey a rule?' — If this is not a question about causes then it is about a justification of my following the rule in the way I do. If I have exhausted the justifications I have reached bedrock and my spade is turned. Then I am entitled to say 'This is simply what I do'.[9]

And again, he wrote:

> When I obey a rule I do not choose, I obey the rule blindly.[10]

The rules of our language are learnt at a very early age and Moore's propositions form part of our picture of the world. They are a presupposition of doubting, knowing and remembering and are taken for granted. However, the propositions Moore listed are not exhaustive and their status can change. Thus 'I have never been to the moon' said a hundred years ago would have a different status to the same claim made today. A hundred years ago, it simply would not have made sense to doubt this statement. Today, by contrast, we could imagine someone replying, 'Really? I thought you were part of the last Apollo mission?'.

Questioning fundamental basic beliefs involves questioning a whole way of looking at the world. There are various ways of looking at the world, and children in different societies can be educated into different forms of life or frameworks of understanding. This is where Wittgenstein's talk of language games comes in. To refer to 'language games' can appear pejorative or to trivialise something profound, but this was not Wittgenstein's intention. A language game gives expression to a form of life, and the language game is integral to the form of life. However, just as there can be different forms of life, so there can be different language games. There may be overlaps between languages games — just as there are overlaps between the rules of rugby and the rules of soccer — but this does not prevent them being widely divergent.

With this as background, we can now return to look at the challenge that anti-realism presents, although quite specifically I will argue in chapter 4 that modern anti-realists misunderstand Wittgenstein and misuse his approach to philosophical problems.

ANTI-REALISM IN RELIGION AND MORALITY

Anti-realism rejects the correspondence theory of truth and maintains that what makes statements true is that they cohere or fit in with other true statements within a given form of life. The idea of justification or foundations for knowledge simply does not, anti-realists claim, make sense. Rather, every form of life has certain ground rules which one is educated to accept and which, within this form of life, it does not make sense to doubt. For instance, until recently in the field of science the idea that natural laws always hold was accepted, as was the idea that there are no inexplicable events and all events have a cause.[1] It was also accepted that the speed of light is an absolute and that time travel is impossible. No-one can prove these to be true, instead they are the basic presuppositions of the scientific form of life and, in the future, it is possible that they may be shown to be false — just as many previously unquestioned assumptions of science have subsequently been rejected.

Take a statement like 'This is a chair'. There is no way this can be proved, instead everyone in our society accepts this because we have been educated into a form of life where we take this for granted. In Roman society, however, no-one would recognises what we call a chair as a chair, because they did not have chairs. In some African tribal societies certain areas are taboo and the spirits control every aspect of the life of the society. When a person dies, they join the other ancestors and individuals can intercede for the help of the spirit ancestors. No-one can prove this to be true (or false), but within the relevant form of life these are unquestionably true.

THE POWER OF EDUCATION

Much depends on the education process and the society into which an individual is born. If, for instance, a person is born in Ireland, they are likely to be a Catholic; if in parts of the South of the United States, a Baptist; if in Greece, a member of the Greek Orthodox Church; if in Iran, a Muslim; if in Thailand, a Buddhist. In South Australia there are a large number of Lutherans because that was where German immigrants to Australia landed. They built Lutheran schools which educated children to be Lutheran and so the process has continued. The same applies to Irish Catholic or to Jewish immigrants into the United States or to Muslims who come to, say, Britain. In each of these and other cases, individuals may be passionately committed to the truths of a particular religion, but this is, it is claimed, a matter of assent to the grammar of belief and the form of life which this grammar expresses. There is no appeal to an independent standard of truth nor indeed, is there any search for ultimate truth.

We, whoever we may be, are inculcated into a framework at our parents' knees and our whole education process serves to confirm this framework. This is one of the reasons for the emphasis placed on education as parents wish their children to be educated into the values that they themselves endorse.

Nowhere is this more clear than in the case of religion where each religious group is anxious that children should attend their own denomination's schools. Thus an Anglican attends an Anglican school and a Muslim an Islamic school. Within these schools, the framework into which the child is being educated is reinforced and they are encouraged to mix with other like minded children. There may well be Lutheran, Anglican, Jewish or Islamic youth clubs where the values and ideas of the group are again reinforced and, frequently, the parents will hope that their children will end up marrying someone from the same faith community. Any children that result will be brought up in this community and so the process is continued from generation to generation. As D.Z. Phillips wrote:

> The child learns to believe a host of things, that is, it learns to act according to these beliefs. Bit by bit, there forms a system of what is believed, and in that system some things stands unshakeably fast and

> some are more or less liable to shift. What stands fast does so, not
> because it is intrinsically obvious or convincing; it is rather held fast
> by what lies around it.[2]

We have here a clear reference to the coherence theory of truth
('what stands fast does so ... [because of] what lies around it'). In
other words, within certain forms of life certain beliefs stand fast
and are held to be true. There is no appeal beyond the framework
— truth *is* what stands fast. Systematic theology explores the grammar of Christian belief — what can and cannot be said within the
form of life of Christianity. In religious terms, what is not acceptable
is heretical.

Anti-realism most specifically does not reject religious belief —
quite the reverse. It maintains that religious beliefs are true, but that
this truth is contained within and validated by a particular form of
life. There are no absolute truths in religion or morality, rather all
truth is internal to the language game being played. As Fergus Kerr[3]
pointed out, Descartes attempted to describe the absolute view of
reality and aimed at a description of things as they would be in our
absence. However, anti-realists reject the possibility of such description or, indeed, of a real world. In part 2 it will be made clear that in
this respect they have something in common with post-modernism.

God exists for anti-realists, but not in the way that a physical
object exists. God, they claim, is not like an undiscovered planet; God
is not an object. It is for this reason, D.Z. Phillips says, that if any
object is claimed to be God, this is idolatry, and Fr Gareth Moore says
'God is nothing, there is nothing that is God'. God is real and the believer relates to the reality of God, but this reality is found within the language game of the believing community and there is no external
referent. If there was such a referent, then because there is no way of
proving that it exists, religious faith would be tentative. Anti-realists
specifically claim that this is not the case. There is an absolute commitment by the believer to the truth of what he or she believes, and
these beliefs *are* true, within the community of believers.

CONVERSION

Imagine that you, as a non-Catholic, decided to marry a Roman
Catholic. You were impressed by his or her commitment and you
loved him or her dearly. You decided on reflection to become a
Catholic. You would attend church with your beloved and eventually

would go and receive instruction from the priest or a trained assistant. You would be taken through the RCIA program (the Roman Catholic program for the Initiation of Adults). You would be taught what you should or should not say, what Catholics believe and how these beliefs are to be understood. You would learn about the sacraments of the Church, the symbols and the obligations of a Catholic. You would be taken through the catechism and would read about the lives of the saints. You would mix with other Catholics at social functions. You might ask questions and these would be answered by reference to the tradition. What would happen, however, if you began to have doubts and said, for instance:

- 'Perhaps Mary was not a virgin. Maybe she had a happy and healthy sex life. After all, Matthew's Gospel says that Joseph did not make love to Mary until after Jesus was born — thus implying that he did after the birth of Jesus.[4] Also the Gospels refer to Jesus' brothers and sisters.'
- 'Why was Mary described as the mother of God? After all the vote to give her this status was taken at Ephesus (the home of the goddess Athena and a place where something equivalent to a female deity would have been widely supported) three hundred years after Jesus' death, and it was taken very quickly and before opposing bishops could arrive. Some opponents were locked up so they could not vote.'
- 'I do not accept the philosophy of Aristotle on which Catholic Natural Theology is based and do not accept that all human beings share a single human nature. I therefore think that homosexuals and lesbians should be free to fulfil their own sexual natures within same sex relationships.'[5]
- 'Why should I believe that Jesus rose embodied from the grave when this seems unlikely, when I can make little sense of the idea of Jesus ascending into heaven and when alternative views of eternal life are available?
- 'Why should I accept the authority of the Pope? He is just another human being whom I respect, but I cannot see why he should be given any particular authority more than any other bishop, given that there have been so many corrupt, evil and wicked Popes in the past and they have made so many mistakes and changes in doctrine. I also do not accept recent changes to Church teaching which seem to elevate opinions of the Pope into an almost infallible status.'

The priest or assistant might try to convince you, but could only do so by reference to the Christian traditions, to the Catholic catechisms, to Catholic writers and to what is accepted within the Catholic community. As Fr Gareth Moore put it:

> ... in religion there is a distinction between grounds and evidence ... That the Pope says contraception is wrong is not *evidence* that it is wrong; but for a Catholic or mainstream Christian it is certainly grounds for believing it is wrong.[6]

In other words, there is no independent (in the sense of free from perspective) evidence for the truth of what Catholicism teaches. Rather, the grounds for believing Catholic truths are simply that these are the truths Catholics accept. Within the Catholic tradition, authority of teaching is of vital importance. Thus as Moore, said:

> ... in all fields a large importance is given to *authority* ... In religion, what is said and done is not to be in conformity with what is established by impartial inquiry, by going and looking at how things are, by experimenting. Rather is it to be conformable to what is *authoritatively said*.[7]

Within the Catholic tradition, what is true is what is held authoritatively within the tradition. Truth, in other words, is based on coherence with other statements within the Catholic form of life and on what the leaders of the Church lay down as orthodoxy. What is false is what is held as false by those who lead the tradition:

> ... it is a feature of religion that people *correct* each other in religious matters, or at least try to. Those people with a more authoritative voice, the leaders, correct the followers ... Now he has a wrong opinion. He has to be corrected, not in the sense of having his mistake pointed out to him ... but in the sense of being persuaded to orthodoxy, won from his error. He has to be taught what is the right thing to say ... In the end the argument of the orthodox may have to come down to saying, 'This just is what the Christian faith is. This is what is believed and is to be believed. Believe this, not that.' It is not that no other position is reasonably tenable, but that no other opinion *is to be held*.[8]

The same will apply in other language games. Assume that a young woman goes to live in Tehran. She meets and falls in love with a young Muslim doctor — intelligent, well educated and devout. Their love blossoms and she is impressed with his prayer life (so much in excess of that found in her own culture) and devotion to Allah. She is also impressed with the commitment of her husband and his friends to charitable works, fasting and their compassion and understanding for those in need. She therefore decides to become a Muslim. She reads the Holy Koran, the Hadith and books written by Muslims. She goes to the mosque and takes instruction from the Imam. The Imam explains the role of the Prophet and the rich tradition of Islam. However, she may then begin to ask questions. Let us say that after a few months of instruction she says:

- 'I believe that Mohammed made up the Koran. Clearly he was an inspired and a great leader, but no more than this. I can see no basis for the claim that the Koran is divinely dictated. After all, his own secretary abandoned faith in him when he suggested passages which Mohammed agreed could be incorporated. Also, the idea of an angel dictating to him seems very far fetched.'
- 'Some passages in the Koran are wonderful, but others seem primitive and uncivilised. No god worth worshipping could advocate some of the punishments in the Koran — they are barbarous. It is a culturally relative document with only limited application today.'
- 'Women are not treated equally in the Koran. I do understand some Islamic societies treat people badly and that this is not in accordance with the Koran, but within the Koran itself women seem to be treated as less than men and I cannot accept this.'
- 'Even if there is a life after death, the picture the Koran paints seems to be male dominated and unfair to women. At most it may have been a picture that Mohammed used to make sense of his ideas, but no more than that.'
- 'I cannot accept the certainty of Islam or the lack of freedom or the conformity that it requires. I think Islam is a basic human story built up round a remarkable man, but no more than that.'

As with the Catholic example given previously, the Imam would not try to prove any of these statements to be false by recourse to some independent evidence. There is none. Rather, he would appeal to the Islamic tradition, to the authorities which are accepted within Islam, and seek to persuade the woman to accept the Islamic perspective which to him, within the form of life, seems so self-evidently true.

In the University of London College in which I lecture, there are dedicated and committed Catholics and Muslims who both see the truths within their forms of life as 'obvious' and unquestioned. The anti-realist will readily explain this by the form of life into which they have been educated. To each group, their own truth claims are self-evident and they will buttress these claims and seek to support them by appeal to literature and individuals within their own tradition. Thus, if a Catholic is disturbed about her faith, she will tend to seek guidance from Catholic friends or a Catholic priest to confirm her in her views. A Muslim student of mine who was disturbed by the difficulties of the claim that 'everything happens by God's will' because this seemed to infringe on human freedom, went to her Imam. The Imam reassured her that there was no difficulty and she must rely on the revelation of God and not seek to question. Anti-realists would see this as a good example of the validity of their views; truth is internal to the framework and the 'authorities' are those which the framework accepts. This is why some religious groups are keen to ensure that young pupils and others are exposed only to their own views of truth and they resist any attempt at dispassionate inquiry. My own college, Heythrop, is a wonderful counter example; while it is a Jesuit institution, it has the strongest commitment to academic excellence.

THE POWER TO INFLUENCE THE STORY

In recent years there has been an increase in the power of the Roman Magisterium with much greater emphasis on the need for Catholics to conform to the beliefs of the Church. In 1991, for the first time, those who were to be ordained to be deacons had to sign an oath giving 'religious assent of will and intellect to all teachings of the Magisterium'. No evidence is given for the truth of these teachings, but they now have to be accepted as true if a man is to be ordained as a deacon.[9] This has never before been required in the Catholic Church but the measure has been introduced to ensure orthodoxy (compliance with what is accepted in the Church). In a similar way, those who teach in Catholic institutions are now required to teach 'in accordance with the teaching of the Magisterium'.

This process is at work in sects and mainstream religions around the world. In Australia, a relatively secular, modern, liberal country, signs of the same process are in evidence. Certain right-wing Australian Catholic bishops lay down teaching strategies in schools in their archdioceses which take seriously the education of children into 'the truth' as they see it, with alternative views being unacceptable. For instance, the Catholic approach to sexuality, abortion or euthanasia will be taught and alternative approaches, even those advocated by scholars in the Catholic tradition, will not be given equal weight or will not be discussed at all. There is an increase in emphasis on orthodoxy, with Catholic groups such as Opus Dei and the Neo Catechuminant movement gaining in influence. In Australia, people such as Archbishop Pell in Melbourne are appointed because they are seen to be guarantors of orthodoxy who will introduce measures to ensure compliance with 'the truth' (the truth accepted within a fairly narrowly defined Catholic form of life). In a similar way in Sydney Anglican Evangelicalism and some others have come to a position of influence where their views on truth can be imposed on others. As a result of their efforts, Anglicanism in Sydney is often seen to be out of keeping with the mainstream Anglican tradition.[10] The Anglican tradition has always prided itself on its breadth and tolerance for a very wide spread of views. However, such is the nature of the Anglican Church, with its lack of a clear centre or any central teaching authority, that individual dioceses can become dominated by extreme groups. These only have to secure majorities in various key committees and bodies to ensure that their views become accepted as orthodoxy. Once control of school curricula, training of priests and lay education is achieved, then it is a relatively simple matter to ensure that the only people appointed are those who agree with the views being espoused by the leaders of particular sectarian movements.

Fundamentalists can succeed whatever the structure of a religious organisation. Where power is concentrated in the centre (as in the case of the Roman Catholic Church) and once the centre and its teaching authority is controlled, the broad life of the religious group can be gradually influenced. Change in this case is not easily achieved as the broad mass of ordinary believers may well resist it and remain faithful to more traditional ideals for some years but, over time, they will change as they are 'taught' the new approach. It may take a generation or more before gradual change can be brought about by the selection of key leaders. In a more dispersed structure (such as that found within Methodism or the Anglican Church), different areas of the world can more readily be controlled although it is more difficult to influence the whole worldwide body of believers. The Lambeth Conference, the ten-yearly meeting of Bishops of the Anglican communion, was effectively 'hijacked' in 1998 by a well organised group of evangelicals to ensure their views on homosexuality prevailed. Few bishops dared speak out against them, some simply abstained or absented themselves from the vote.

None of these fundamentalist influence groups work by appeal to some objective truth which can be justified to a non-sympathetic observer. Instead, they are clear that they have the truth. They appeal to writers that support their pre-formed views and seek by various means to disseminate their views. Money, effective use of the media and passionate oratory are all employed, but rarely cool, dispassionate argument. Truth, then, becomes a matter of persuading people into one's framework. The justification for doing this is one's conviction that one is right as well as the shared conviction of one's group.

THE DEVELOPMENT OF STORIES

If the history of major religions is examined it can be seen that the stories by which believers live have evolved over time. For instance, the Christian stories about Jesus grew out of a Hebrew background, from which Jesus himself came. The stories were passed down by word of mouth and various sources were then combined into written form. Evidence was sought and selected which would point to Jesus being the Messiah foretold in the Hebrew Scriptures (even though many passages were never intended to be used in the way the early Christian writers used them). Eventually, some, not all, of these stories were chosen for inclusion in the 'Canon' of the New Testament. Over the next five centuries, various Councils or meetings of the Church were held to decide which views were 'orthodox' and which were 'heretical'. These decisions were taken by majority vote of those who attended. The ideas which received majority support were accepted and declared as orthodox, while the ideas that lost out were rejected and termed 'heretical'. They were then stamped out, often by severe means.[11] Thus the 'story' of Christianity and ideas such as redemption, atonement, salvation, Trinity, Mary as the mother of God and the role of the Church were built up over time. What was true then became what was accepted within the 'official story' laid down by the Church and if anyone seriously challenged this, sanctions were brought to bear to exclude them. All this fits in perfectly with an anti-realist understanding of religious belief and religious truth claims.

Revelation appears to be a difficult topic for the anti-realist to deal with, but again an explanation is given. Because anti-realists deny any claim to a transcendent order or any realist claim to reference, they reject claims that God reveals certain things. Indeed given the number of competing claims to revelation in different religions, they say that no appeal to revelation can be made unless grounds can be given as to why one revelation should be chosen rather than another. This is why anti-realists reject Reformed Epistemology. Instead, within each religious story, they see certain claims as being given a privileged character, and 'revelation' is the word used by believers in the group in question to validate the status of these claims.

Conversion from one framework to another is possible. For instance, a person may have grown up in a particular religious tradition and the form of life that, as Wittgenstein put it, may grow old. The person may recognise that they are living in a shell, saying words or taking part in church services that no longer have real meaning for them. Numerous priests come to this position, realising that they no longer believe the words they say. They may then be faced with the stark choice to give up their priesthood when they are trained for no other job, when it would mean loneliness, isolation and loss of financial security at a stage in life when all these are important factors, or to continue in a shell in which they no longer believe. For such individuals, anti-realism can provide a way forward as they come to see that they are part of a community and what the language or worship may express is identification with this community. They then come to see a renewed value in worship and liturgy as it helps to create meaning for people for whom no other meaning would exist. An alternative may be to convert to another framework which the individual feels is more intellectually or emotionally satisfying. However, such a conversion is not usually based on any philosophic proof or analysis. Instead, it rests on a change of outlook, on coming to see things in a different way.

Truth, then, according to the anti-realist view, is based on coherence within a particular form of life. We are educated into seeing the world in a certain way and what is true depends on the framework within which we operate. Within Islam it is true that a man may have four wives, while within Christianity it is morally acceptable to have one. Within the official teaching of Catholicism artificial birth control is unacceptable and immoral (the present Pope having said that contraception is as grave a sin as abortion), while Protestant and Orthodox Christians consider it as morally acceptable. There is no independent standard of truth and the community is the final arbiter.

It is not only within philosophy that the idea of truth as a construct is now widely accepted. Within psychology the same trend is at work, and this will be explored in the next chapter.

5

CONSTRUCTIVISM IN PSYCHOLOGY

FREUD AND JUNG

In the popular mind, Freud and Jung are still the best known figures in the world of psychology and psychoanalysis, although many
psychologists today do not take them seriously. This is, at least in
part, due to the fact that the theories of both Freud and Jung are
theories which are not subject to empirical verification, and in the
field of experimental psychology the ability to verify theories is considered to be of central importance.

Freud is popularly known for his emphasis on the importance of
dreams and of repressed conflicts (sexuality) in many of the problems that men and women face. He also allowed no place for God.

Jung is more popular among many of those with religious lean-
ings because he seems to have left room for God in a way which
Freud did not. Jung was sympathetic to theism but not a theist. He
had an outspoken sympathy for Christianity, yet he was also critical
of it. He saw religion as the 'attitude peculiar to a consciousness
which has been altered by the experience of numinosum'. Jung
defined the term 'numinous immediate experience' as a happening
which bestows on a person a sudden insight into another dimension
and which affects the person's whole being. This is a positive view
that religion gave humanity, an integrated view of the world and of
ourselves in it, giving meaning and direction in life. Such experiences are the powerful, transforming experiences that lift a person

out of the world only to plunge them back into it, giving them a new way of seeing and feeling things and a new set of marching orders. For Jung, integration of the different aspects of one's personality was a central part of coping with psychological difficulties and with the challenges that life brings in its different stages. This integration involved an inner journey in which the different facets of the self were brought together.

A positive religious understanding of the world enabled the cultivation and enjoyment of that which is most precious and positive to a person. By contrast, a negative mode of religion was fearful attention being paid to that which we are frightened by, such as spirits, powers and demons. In either case, these experiences, according to Jung, happen to us and cannot be caused by us. They are a cause external to the individual causing a peculiar alteration of consciousness.

William James makes the same point when he claims that mystical experiences occur to a person; they cannot be sought. The person is essentially passive. Jung does not confuse such experiences with sentimentality (a sad state of mind, of reminiscences, mild passive yearning for a better state of affairs). He had a positive evaluation of religion for psychological health and said that among all his patients who were over the age of 35, there was not one whose problem in the last resort was not that of finding a religious outlook on life. James was certain that every one of them fell ill because they had lost that which the living religions of every age have given to their followers. Not one of his patients was really healed who did not in some way regain his or her religious outlook.

Jung argued that the absence of religion was responsible for many neuroses. He considered that the deepest part of the psyche was transpersonal, a common possession of all humanity. The 'collective unconscious' is composed of archetypes which are potential patternings for the development of personality. The archetypes are seeds of the self, sources of energy available for an individual's growth into wholeness. The archetypes are unconscious. They are experienced through symbols which express the archetypes and make their energy available for integration into conscious personality. The psyche expresses depth experiences first of all in images which are symbolic expressions of the experiences, and then in concepts which represent a secondary-level thinking. St Teresa of Avila's work is an example of this.

ST TERESA OF AVILA

St Teresa's *The Interior Castle* is a mystical work where St Teresa describes the journey of the soul from the exterior of the castle to the interior where God lives. She describes her own prayer experiences as a series of transformations culminating in a spiritual union with Christ. The journey involves passing through six dwelling places before arriving at the centre, the seventh. The castle is global so the dwelling places are global, spheres within a sphere.

The journey involves two movements, which she likens to the efforts needed to fill troughs of water. Prayer in the first three dwellings is active, like filling a trough through a series of aqueducts. Prayer for the last three dwellings is like receptive prayer of contemplation, like a trough near its source being easily filled. The fourth dwelling is a transitional phase from active to passive. *The Interior Castle* is a story set in an old castle which is entered by a 'soul', the heroine, who journeys through the castle. The outer environs of the castle are cold, dark and unpleasant but as the soul enters the depths of the castle the atmosphere changes; darkness gives way to light, and the air becomes warmer. Each of the dwelling places is a world in itself but the centre has a magnetic attraction and lures the heroine forward. For St Teresa, the whole is an inner journey representing growing union with Christ

The first three stages require the individual to be involved in an active prayer life and the effort has to be made to enter into a serious prayer relationship. The stages are as follows:

Stage 1: The material things in the world provide a very real distraction. They are seen as being central to the life of the individual and it is hard to place God at the centre.

Stage 2: The experience of a call from God deepens. This comes through other people, as well as periods of trial, suffering, dissatisfaction with the world and reading books. It is in this stage that the individual begins to cease centring on themselves and a genuine start is made on the journey towards God.

Stage 3: By this stage, prayer is a central and integral part of the person's life. The person is stable but they also feel a call to move on. It is necessary in this stage to deepen prayer life or else all vitality and energy for the journey will be lost here.

Stage 4: This is the intermediary stage, the middle one of the seven stages. It is one of transition. In this stage, the individual becomes more passive in prayer and a real faith and confidence in the service of God start to emerge. St Teresa portrays this by two fonts with two water troughs. One trough is filled via aqueducts requiring skill and ingenuity (these represent prayer begun by the person and ending with God) while the second is filled directly from the spring and is always flowing (this represents prayer that begins with God and ends in the person). This fourth stage is the beginning of true mysticism.

Stage 5: The fifth stage sees an experience of union with God — dying in Christ and rising to new life like the caterpillar that dies to be born as a butterfly.

Stage 6: This stage represents intensification of the union between the individual and God, a time of betrothal and purification, a stage of pain and joy.

Stage 7: The seventh stage is one of union with God. 'One can say no more — in so far as can be understood — than that the soul, I mean the spirit, is made one with God.' A deep interior peace is a constant state and one is propelled back into the world. 'This is the reason for prayer ... the birth always of good works.'

St Teresa's imagery is related to a collective layer of the psyche and can therefore act as a guide to meanings that are not the sole possession of a sixteenth-century nun. They can be claimed to provide a guide to the psyche across time and culture. They stand as an example of the inner journey towards what she considered was a reality found deep within herself. Apart from the image of the castle, St Teresa also uses images of water, journey, serpents, devils, butterfly, marriage and Christ. She has been called a psychological mystic because her journey to God is also a journey to the inner self, a movement to God which involves self-knowledge. To have union with God at the centre is to possess one's life more fully. Her subtle descriptions of inner experiences provide a map of human development and religious conversion.

If Jung's theory is accepted, St Teresa's images are the expression of her inner experiences. The words she uses to describe her inner experiences are a secondary mode of communication. Her images are symbols, expressions of meanings which can only be partially articulated. Jung, like St Teresa, considered that human beings have to go on an inner journey to find themselves because their true selves lie cloaked beneath masks in the depths of the psyche. Many resist this inner journey and are content to live on the surface of their selves and, therefore, they do not become self-aware. Only those who take the inner journey, and thus who are not solely preoccupied with the outer world, are able to achieve wisdom and understanding about themselves.

The archetypes are at least partly a construction based on our common humanity, and they are claimed to be found in all human beings. (Many modern films give expression to the Jungian archetypes which is why they resonate so much with audiences as they touch something which is readily recognisable.) The inner journey culminates, for Jung, in the archetypes, but Jung is ambiguous as to the status of the archetypes and, particularly, as to whether these are ultimate brute facts located in the depths of the human psyche or whether they are an 'imprint' of a divine reality beyond. Jung considered that this was a question that psychology could not answer, although it was a question he could never leave alone.

We have here a direct parallel with the issue of realism and antirealism, namely, is the reality of God or that which is ultimate to be found in something we construct within the human community in which we live or is it something which we discover, possibly by undertaking an inner journey in the way of St Teresa of Avila or St John of the Cross? It would be easy to see how St Teresa's description of her experiences could be regarded as evidence of the reality she had constructed on the basis of her religious world view and the background into which she had been educated and which she had appropriated for herself. She talks of castles and courtyards, aqueducts and heroines, all very much a product of the culture of her time. The issue, then, is not whether her descriptions of what she experienced were real — there is no doubt that they were — but the issue is whether the reality is one that she discovered within herself or a reality which she constructed. It can be seen that this challenges one's view of what it means for an experience to be real. Reality can be constructed and, indeed, many psychologists today would say that all reality is constructed and that mental health problems often arise because of unhelpful constructs.

Jung and the great mystics of the past emphasised the importance of the inner journey to seek the truth about oneself, truth that was grounded in a common anthropology, a common understanding of what it is to be human. However in the 1920s there was a move in psychology away from the psychoanalytic tradition of Freud and Jung to a psychology based on observation. Psychology desired to become more scientific and less speculative, testing its hypotheses using scientific method and employing rational principles of sceptical inquiry. It therefore became positivistic, claiming that if the conclusions were not based on sound method and evidence, we had no reason to accept them. Moreover, most psychologists today are more interested in what 'most people do most of the time' and see this as a better place to start the study of mental life and behaviour than the patients in psychiatric care. Psychologists particularly under the influence of John Watson argued that the only objective feature that we could study scientifically was behaviour. Behaviourists therefore did not seek to ask what went on inside people's heads or the influence of early experience but instead studied the observable world of actions.

A famous example of behaviourism is Pavlov's dogs. The Russian psychologist Ivan Pavlov fed dogs in his laboratory at a certain time and simultaneously rang a bell. After repeated presentation of the food when the bell was rung, the bell was then rung but no food appeared. Because the dogs had learned to associate the bell and food, their saliva flowed on hearing the bell. Over time the dogs had been 'conditioned' and had paired the bell and the food: the stimulus (the bell) produced the reaction (salivation). This analysis was called stimulus–response theory.

It was found that learned behaviour could also be 'unlearned', and this became known as learning theory. Its later subsequent developments, particularly under B.F. Skinner, represented major advances in our understanding of human behaviour. It has been extensively developed as a way of modifying behaviour and behavioural problems, and remains, for example, the most effective means of treating phobias.

A.T. BECK

By the 1960s many psychologists were dissatisfied with behaviourism. Under the influence of the linguist Noam Chomsky the 'cognitive revolution' took place, a paradigm shift which viewed the internal working of the mind as a legitimate object of scientific inquiry. Simply put, one of the effects was to focus on the intervening organism between the stimulus and response. Thus:

Stimulus ➝ Organism (human being) ➝ Response

The organism (person) 'mediates' the response, and our responses can differ according to internal differences, particularly in terms of our beliefs, interpretations and memories. The American psychiatrist A.T. Beck, from observation of his patients and their thoughts and beliefs, came to conclude that it is not so much events (stimuli) that trouble us, as the interpretation that we put upon them. Along with other theorists and practitioners he developed 'cognitive therapy' as a means of treating, initially, depression and anxiety, and now a wide range of emotional disorders.

Imagine that you are walking down the street and you see a friend on the other side. You wave but there is no response. The thought goes through your mind that 'she's ignoring me. I must have done something to upset her.' If this friend is important to you, you may feel worried or upset by this event. If, however, you think 'She hasn't got her glasses on and probably didn't see me' or 'She must be preoccupied by something and didn't notice me', your reaction is likely to be very different. Beck found that in his depressed patients their interpretations were systematically negative, extreme and unrealistic. Moreover, people would actually distort events to make them fit with their pre-existing beliefs, or 'schemas' as he called them.

So much depends on the individual and the framework assumptions he or she brings to bear on the experience. Imagine a woman walking home across a neglected and deserted graveyard at night. She has been watching the film *Psycho* and suddenly sees a shadow looming towards her very quickly. She might think this is a rapist, scream and run for her life. Now assume that another woman has just been to a martial arts class and has just completed her black belt in judo. She sees the shadow and interprets this as a male attacker. She may relish the excitement of being able to throw someone over the adjacent gravestones and may therefore turn and walk towards the shadow, looking forward to the encounter. A third woman may have been forced to walk across the graveyard as she is late for a meeting, and to go round would take too long. She has a fear of ghosts and is convinced that the shadow is some form of ghost coming to enslave her. Her reaction may be one of paralysis and abject terror. In the three cases the stimulus (event or situation) has been interpreted in different ways. Where is the truth? What appears as true to one person is not the same to another. Much depends on the way events are interpreted and the view of reality that is constructed.

Beck found that in his patients there were underlying 'core schema' which caused and maintained the emotional problems they experienced. These beliefs tend to be unconditional and negative, and there are surprisingly few of them. Very common examples seen almost daily in the clinical work of cognitive therapists include, 'I am no good', 'I am worthless', 'I am bad', 'I am unlovable', 'I am useless', 'I am weak', 'I am a nobody' and 'I am a failure'. Where there is a wide variation is in the way we deal with these core beliefs. So, for example, one person who believes that they are a failure may strive to 'disprove' this by becoming very successful and rich in business, but remains very vulnerable to any form of failure, perceived or actual. Another person may 'live out' the belief by never taking on anything where there is a risk of failing and thus underachieve and 'confirm' the belief. These are two very different forms of behaviour stemming from the same core schema.

Beck took a realist approach to truth and much of the focus of the cognitive approach focuses on how accurate the person is in interpreting their experience. A principle means of examining schema is by reviewing the evidence for and against the belief, by considering if it would stand up in court. In the light of this, people are helped to construct beliefs that are more accurate, realistic and helpful to them in living their lives.

G.A. Kelly took a different approach claiming that reality is simply an internal construct, an internal set of beliefs and filters which help us to organise and order reality.

The point is that how we think is vital. Many of our thoughts will be automatic and give rise to our reactions and understanding. Coming to terms with HOW we think is an essential part of understanding truth. On both these views, truth is radically dependent on the reality we construct.

CONSTRUCTED REALITY

It is generally agreed in psychology that the early years and early relationships have a crucial impact on a person's life and personality. We draw conclusions about ourselves, other people, the world we live in and our place in it on the basis of our experience. In the early years what we are told and how we are treated by our parents, our family and other important adults such as teachers determines the type of 'map' that we draw. If a child is not praised, loved and valued, feels safe or lives in a stable, predictable environment, they may well draw negative conclusions about themselves.

A young child whose father dies may comes to think that these events have happened because they have been naughty and thus they can take the blame on themselves. If they are not given any reassurance or more accurate explanation of why this happens, they may conclude that 'Daddy got ill because I was naughty, so I killed Daddy. I must be bad.' This will, naturally, affect the way they see not just themselves but also the world and how they relate to other people. They will see their endeavours as not being valued. They may throw themselves into work, be kind to people or be good hoping that no-one will 'discover' what they are 'really' like. Intimacy becomes difficult and dangerous because of the risk of being 'found out'. They may develop masks which they think will make them more acceptable and more lovable. They will not be aware of doing this but the construct of reality they have produced will result in them seeing the world in a certain way. These then form compensatory beliefs (for example, the importance of virtue, goodness or working hard) and these, again, form part of the filter through which they see the world. Truth, then, becomes filtered through individual perspectives and the task of the therapist is to help his or her patient to adjust their view of reality so that it becomes a view that they can live with and which helps them to adjust to the world and to flourish.

This last sentence contains an important assumption, namely, that to function well in the world and to flourish are the highest objectives of human life and that they provide the ultimate criteria for the ways in which judgments about reality are to be made. This is, at the least, a debatable assumption. Someone who is well balanced, happy and stress free may function well in the world, but they may also not be seeing life in any truthful sense. The fact that life seems good, that one is happy and the world is an attractive place may be based on a self-deceit that goes to the core of one's being. It may represent a refusal to face reality that is endemic and deep seated.

CONSTRUCTING LIES

According to cognitive theory, we are organisms that need to make sense of our experience ('the will to meaning') and construct the models of reality in which we live, and thus the truths by which we live function as 'our reality'. An example may illustrate the way that reality may be constructed by governments to persuade people to see the world in which they live in a certain way. The following is extracted from an article on Chile in the British newspaper, the *Independent*, on Sunday, 13 December 1998. It describes how ordinary Chileans saw the overthrow of their democratically elected president by a general who we now know was financed and supported by Western interests, particularly the United States. His regime was responsible for the systematic murder and torture of tens of thousands of people in the most brutal and extreme manner. The ordinary people were manipulated so that they came to welcome the *mano duro* (the hard fist) of the General:

> Like the vast majority of Chileans, the Montes family are too busy working to feed, clothe and educate their children. Like the vast majority of Chileans they long ago accepted General Pinochet as part of their political system, not only the coup leader (against the former President Allende) but the one who handed over his power to democracy ... 'Everyone knew that Allende wanted the poor people to live better. He wanted the poor to have clothes on their back, he wanted them to eat meat' said Alicia, Cesar's mother. 'The rich didn't like that. So they started to sabotage him. They hoarded food. Shop shelves were empty, yet people saw lorries dumping good potatoes into ditches at night. They had factories, electric pylons blown up, so they could say "Look what a bad President he is." We had to get up at five in the morning and queue for hours just to get bread. I couldn't get food for my kids, so I started to blame the government. Plus, there was a lot of looting as people got hungrier. I know a lot of women who deliberately stopped having children because they didn't know whether they could provide for them. When Pinochet staged the coup, we felt sorry for Allende, we knew that it was the rich who had screwed him, but there was a sense of hope.'

'They shut down all radio and TV except the military channel, which said that Allende had committed suicide' she went on. 'Nobody believed it. In his last radio broadcast, he said that he would not come out alive. The most likely thing is that he fought to the last moment. If he'd committed suicide, they'd have shown his body as proof.' General Pinochet imposed a total curfew for three days, restricting people to their homes. That is why, the Montes said, those unaffected were not aware that leftists were disappearing. 'Then all the food reappeared so that the poor were happy' said Alicia. 'Since we were not involved, we didn't know what was happening. But one day a neighbour came by and said she had seen bodies being loaded into a military lorry. Then another neighbour's brother-in-law disappeared. There was a lot of fear ...'

The picture painted here is repeated throughout the world. Whether in Hitler's German, in Pol Pot's Cambodia, in Rwanda, Bosnia, Serbia or even in the 'free' West, people are manipulated or deceived into a picture of reality which has nothing to do with truth. The media, which is controlled, constructs reality for them and social conditions are created which enable this constructed reality to be acceptable and even seen as desirable. However, what is constructed is a lie, and just because people may be content with being deceived does not mean that they are any the less deceived.

Even in the so-called free West, the media and marketing executives encourage people to find meaning and value in acquiring goods and living a certain lifestyle, and the fact that people live this lifestyle is portrayed as having happiness. This vision of reality is a constructed vision, but rather than it being one that each person constructs for him or herself, it is a construction that is subtly imposed by media and government. If one succeeds in convincing oneself to accept or allows oneself to be convinced to accept such constructions, however, it does not mean that one has found truth. It may merely mean that one has been very effective in persuading oneself to accept an illusion because the pain of the human situation may be too unpleasant to face. There is no guarantee, therefore, that happiness and contentment provide any sure route to truth; they may on some occasions provide a route to self-deceit. The very phrase 'deceit' is equated with a lie which is the opposite of truth. And to live a lie, even though it may be a comfortable lie, is still to live a lie.

CONSTRUCTING GOD

Many of the greatest philosophers and writers have been troubled individuals, and, for many of these, their 'trouble' has been that they were wrestling with the realities of life, suffering and evil. To be troubled is not necessarily to be deceived, but it may be to see the world truthfully and to be troubled by it to the core of one's being. This is the very opposite of dogmatic certainty. One refuge for people who feel themselves inadequate may be to retreat to religious certainties and to use these as constructs whereby they can make sense of their world and live in it peacefully and successfully. Again, however, the fact that such frameworks may be successful in helping someone to cope with reality does not mean that they provide any sure guide to truth. The books and the subsequent films *One Flew Over the Cuckoo's Nest* and *The Fisher King* raise the question of who is mad and who is sane. It is too simple to think that those who conform with the world and who are apparently successful and well balanced see the world truthfully. The reverse may be the case.

Psychological constructivists maintain that all beliefs and experience have an internal representation in the form of a construct or schema, including the people we know and ideas of ultimate value. God, therefore, is one construct amongst many others. For instance God may be constructed as a father figure who is loving and kind or a father figure who is stern and judgmental in place of a father who exhibited these qualities and who for some reason is no longer around.

The parallels between constructivism in psychology and anti-realism in philosophy are very clear; in both cases reality is constructed. In psychology, reality is constructed internally by the individual. This provides the filter through which we interpret events. In philosophy, reality is what we construct and truth is what coheres or is accepted within the framework we occupy. In both cases, what is denied is that there is any ultimate truth at stake.

6

THE SCENE IS SET

The scene is set! The claims to reference by realists, whether by religious supporters of Natural Theology, Reformed Epistemo-logists or those who hold to moral absolutes, are based on weak grounds and none provide rational justification for any claim to reference. The idea of truth being relative to the community in which one lives, on the other hand, seems highly plausible. There are no clear rational underpinnings for any specific religious or moral belief. The claim to inner certainty or to privileged access to truth through revelation founders on the rock of multiple truth claims. Almost every religion appeals to 'revelation' yet there seems to be no independent standard against which any such claim can be validated. Anti-realism in philosophy and constructivism in psychology seem to provide a cogent way forward. We are left in a sea of relativism to which post-modernism has contributed in a more extreme way.[1]

In the film *Contact*, Ellie (played by Jodi Foster) is a scientist who first discovers a signal from intelligent life in space. At the beginning of the film she accepts nothing but hard scientific evidence. She appeals to Occam's razor and says:

> *All things being equal, the simplest explanation has to be the right one ... Which is more likely? An All powerful, mysterious God created the universe and then decided not to give any proof of his existence or that he simply does not exist at all and we created him so we would not have to feel so small and alone.*

In the film, Palmer, a theologian and advisor to the President of the United States and a friend of Ellie, says to her:

I wouldn't want to live in a world in which God didn't exist.

Ellie asks in return:

But how do you know you're not deluding yourself.

It is a good question. In fact, it is a vital question and the task of this book is partly to respond to it. It is a question about the nature of truth. The anti-realist and constructivist challenges are persuasive but before replying to them, these challenges need to be developed further by looking at the background to post-modernism, some versions of which fit so well with anti-realism. The next section will start with Kant and will follow one pathway that opens up after his work and will show how it leads from 'the death of God' on to radical relativism.

PART TWO

THERE IS
NO TRUTH
OUT THERE

In the first section it was argued that Natural Theology fails to establish reference to God and so, likewise, does Reformed Epistemology. The only rational alternative seems to be anti-realism which has considerable explanatory power and which avoids the need for a claim to reference while still maintaining truth claims, albeit within different forms of life. The idea of truth being relative to different forms of life seems to be supported by constructivism in psychology. In both cases, therefore, truth is relative to the human community. In this section, this analysis will be extended and it will be argued that a divide in the road after Immanuel Kant has led to a widespread present view of the meaninglessness of life and the search for truth being seen as folly. Post-modernism, in different forms, has value and has revealed important insights but, in some versions, it has undermined confidence in crucial areas of human life. This represents a primary challenge both to education and to the way human beings see themselves.

7

ONTOLOGY AND
EPISTEMOLOGY

Today, more than ever, the search for truth seems to be folly. A number of movements have come together which would seem to justify the view that there is no absolute truth and that truth is radically multiple.

In the **philosophy of religion**, a growing tide of supporters of anti-realism see truth as internal to the language game being played or the story being told. Religious truths, it is held, are not discovered; they are made. Religious truths are essentially truths internal to a fictitious story.

In **mainstream analytic philosophy** we see a general acceptance of the view that the search for any metaphysical underpinning for truth is folly. Since the work of Wittgenstein, the search for firm foundations for knowledge or for any metaphysical underpinning has been almost entirely abandoned.

In **ethics and aesthetics**, what is right and wrong, what is beautiful and ugly, is widely accepted as depending on culture and tradition and having no reality independent of such settings. As Hamlet put it, 'There is nothing good or bad but thinking makes it so.'

Post-modernism rejects any single truth and sees it as being entirely dependent on the viewpoint from which truth is seen.

This section will consider the divide in the road after Immanuel Kant, but before doing so it is necessary to be clear on the nature of the debate about ontology and epistemology.

It is important to separate two issues:

1. *The ontological issue*: Whether there is a world that is independent of the way we experience it — a 'real' world which determines whether our theories about the world are correct.
2. *The epistemological issue*: Whether we can have access to this 'real' world, assuming that it exists.

Various attempts have been made to address the issue of what is real (the ontological issue) and what we know (the epistemological issue). Today there is a general reluctance on the part of many philosophers to discuss the metaphysical or ontological issue. They wish to dismiss all talk of 'things in themselves' or 'the world independent of the way we experience it'. However, on examination, they do not specifically address the issue of WHY we should dismiss or disregard discussion of the world as it is in itself. Rather, they tend to move from the difficulty of knowing about such a world to disregarding or rejecting it.

It may be helpful to define some terms at the outset.

The ontological realist — one who claims that there is a real world, whether we can know it or not. There are two epistemological positions:

1. *Epistemological realism* claims that the real world is accessible and that we can have knowledge which presents it as it is. This falls under ontological realism because it assumes there is a real world.
2. *Epistemological idealism* denies this, claiming that what we know is not the real world as it is in itself. This falls under ontological realism because it assumes there is a real world, even if minds are the ultimate reality in this world which construct or at least radically filter the world as it is.

The ontological idealist — by contrast to the ontological realist, one who maintains that there is no real world other than the one that is created by or dependent on experience. Bishop George Berkeley was an idealist who maintained that the whole material world is mind dependent — the world we experience is actually dependent on, and the creation of, minds. A well known rhyme written by Ronald Knox in the *Times* of London illustrates Berkeley's position well:

> There once was a man who said God,
> Must find it exceedingly odd,
> To see that the tree ceases to be
> When there's no-one about in the quad

Knox clearly had in mind the view that, if to exist is to be perceived, then if there is no-one looking at the tree it would cease to exist. However, a letter in the next day's issue of the paper provided an answer:

> Dear Sir,
> Your astonishments odd.
> I am always about in the quad.
> And that's why the tree
> continues to be
> since perceived by
> Yours faithfully,
> God.

The point is that if God is always looking down at the world, the idealist can claim that the world is maintained in existence by God's sustaining gaze. However intriguing Berkeley's speculations, there are few ontological idealists today. Surprisingly, even ontological realism is now widely rejected, and to understand why this situation has arisen it is necessary to go back to Kant.

IMMANUEL KANT

Kant (1724–1804) shared a common view that God was needed to guarantee human knowledge of reality. Classical metaphysics argued first to God and, because God was held to exist, confidence in the ability of human beings to know the world as it really is was sustained. Kant, although this was not his intention, was responsible for taking away this underpinning.

Kant never left his home town of Konigsberg in Germany but his influence has been greater than any other philosopher in the last four hundred years. He had a high opinion of his own work, claiming to have solved all the major problems of philosophy.

Kant is sometimes described as representing a 'Copernican revolution' in philosophy. Just as Copernicus revolutionised the place we give to the planet Earth in the cosmos by showing that the Earth is a planet which goes around the Sun, Kant is held to have revolutionised philosophy by showing that the order of the world as we see it is dependent on the human observer and the categories we impose. Kant himself had made a contribution to Newton's understanding of the cosmos by showing that through physical forces that were demonstrable, the Sun and the planets have assumed the positions as set out by Copernicus and Kepler. Kant[1] was convinced of the importance of science and empirical observation in enabling us to understand the world *as we experience it*, but it is the world as we experience it that science explains, not the world as it is in itself.

Kant accepted that there is an ontologically independent world, the world of things in themselves, and in virtue of this he is an ontological realist. However, he said that the real world, independent of the form of all experience, is not the world as we know it, and this is the epistemological idealism which runs alongside his ontological realism.

Kant emphasised that human beings do not experience things as they are, rather they experience things at they appear to us. Human beings bring to their understanding of the world certain basic categories such as causation and, even more important, time and space in terms of which we experience the universe. Space and time are intuitions we have based on our common humanity — we have an awareness of space and time and through this we experience the world. This was a major shift of focus as prior to Kant space and time had been considered to be real in themselves. Kant denied this.

Kant's position involves two claims:

1. *A realist ontological* claim that there is a thing in itself, that is, there is a noumenal world which exists independent of what we perceive.
2. *An idealist epistemological* claim that this noumenal world is not the world of which we have knowledge. We can only know the phenomenal world, the world as it appears to us through the spectacles of space and time.

Kant's philosophy has been very much alive throughout the twentieth century, with philosophers such as Brian Magee saying that we can only know things in '... the subjectively determined modes of our own thinking and not as they are in themselves'.[2]

The great advantage of Kant's approach is that it enables us to say that there is a real world, the noumenal world, even thought we cannot know what it is like independent of the way we perceive it. All we can know is the world as we perceive it to be, but what the world is really like in itself is in principle unknowable. Effectively, Kant said that we can forget about the world as it really is independent of the way it is perceived. We can concentrate on knowing the world as we perceive it to be and nothing else is relevant to us. Nevertheless, the real world lurks out there, somehow, independent of our perceptions, and the worry is that what we take to be true may only be the result of our perceptions.

One of the most significant factors in Kant's approach was that it allowed science free reign to explain the phenomenal world, the world of experience, the world as it appears to us. However, his approach also left room for religious faith. Although Kant rejected all attempts to prove the existence of God, it did not mean that Kant did not believe in God. Quite the contrary. His approach left the religious appeal to faith entirely intact as faith was concerned with the noumenal world; it was concerned with God and the inner selves of human beings which are not subject to empirical investigation. Kant rejected all metaphysics. As he stated: 'Metaphysics is a dark and shoreless ocean, marked by no beacons.'[3]

Kant rejected all attempts to prove the existence of God, but God could nevertheless be postulated as a result of:

1. human knowledge of the moral demand, and
2. trust in the ultimate fairness of the universe.

Kant's denial of any possible knowledge of God does not mean that he rejects God. As he said: 'I have therefore found it necessary to deny knowledge, in order to make room for faith.'[4]

Kant's rejection of metaphysics led to theology being seen as a futile exercise which could not yield knowledge of God. Alexander Pope put it clearly:

> Know then thyself,
> presume not God to scan.
> The proper study of Mankind is Man.[5]

The move away from metaphysics left the phenomenal world, the world of human beings, the only one available for study.

Everything else was seen as being irrelevant — even though, for Kant, the noumenal world certainly existed. Acceptance of his view led away from theology as revealing anything about ultimate reality and instead put the emphasis on science as the way we can make sense of the phenomenal world in which we live.

It would be easy to portray Kant as rejecting God entirely and leaving no place for God's activity. This would be a false conclusion, however. God was, indeed, central for Kant. Apart from God's role in ensuring the justice of the universe and that human beings received their just deserts after death, in Kant's view there is one key area of God's activity: moral regeneration. This is often not recognised today. Kant emphasised human autonomy and human rationality — except in one area.

For the French philosopher Jean Rousseau, the 'one great enemy' was the Christian doctrine of original sin. In many ways Kant can be seen to agree with Rousseau in his emphasis on human reason, and yet Kant has a view on evil which comes close to that of St Augustine's. In *Religion Within the Limits of Reason Alone* Kant talked of radical evil almost like original sin. The German poet Goethe had his unflattering suspicions as to why Kant developed this view. He said:

> Kant had criminally smeared his philosopher's cloak with the shameful stain of radical evil, after it had taken him a long human life to cleanse it from many a dirty prejudice ...

'Radical evil' implies that reason turns against its own best interests and that there seems to be a limit to freedom which can place human beings into a bondage. They become fixed in their character because of their past actions and are unable to release themselves. This is not the view most people expect of Kant as most people think Kant worked within the limits of reason alone. This is not the case, however, as Kant left space for faith by separating the phenomenal from the noumenal worlds. Radical evil occurs when human beings freely choose an evil maxim for their actions by subordinating the moral and rational demand to the sensual. To put it another way, evil occurs when the transcendent self is subjugated to the empirical self. Kant talked of the 'conflict of the good with the evil principle for sovereignty over man' leading eventually to the 'victory of the good over the evil principle'.[6]

Kant did not think that any subjugation of the rational to the sensual is ever final; there is always the possibility of moral regeneration. Kant considered that we have an original predisposition to good together with a natural propensity to evil. When Kant talked of 'predisposition' he was talking about basic human nature prior to the exercise of freedom. *Kant considered that we 'make ourselves' as individuals.* Goodness or evil in human beings are the result of what we naturally do with our propensities. These propensities are part of our nature, but it is our free choice to decide what to do with them. This view of our propensity to evil is very similar to the Christian doctrine of original sin. Michalson in his book *Fallen Freedom*[7] finds this the most surprising part of Kant's philosophy.

Kant's chief problem was that he wanted to claim that radical evil is *both* freely elected *and* innate. Kant considers that we freely will our way into bondage to evil — once the propensity is freely chosen, then moral culpability attends the choice. Once we have become evil, we have become dominated by our sensuous nature; and not our rational nature, *we cannot release ourselves by ourselves.* The real problem, therefore, is how Kant saw the possibility of moral regeneration.

MORAL REGENERATION

Kant made two seemingly contradictory claims:

1. Once an individual succumbs to radical evil, then regeneration cannot occur.
2. 'At the same time it must be possible to overcome evil since it occurs in man, a being whose actions are free.'[8]

Most surprisingly, Kant seemed to assume that some form of divine aid is required in order to produce moral regeneration. As he put it:

> Moral regeneration must be within our power; even though what WE are able to do is in itself inadequate and though we thereby only render ourselves susceptible to higher, and for us inscrutable assistance.[9]

Effectively, therefore, radical evil corrupts human beings so that they cannot regenerate themselves of their own accord even though a lingering 'potential for goodness' remains which needs some form of intervention to actualise it.

This is extraordinary, and most writers on Kant do not recognise it, as it seems that Kant moved to a much more traditional

Christian view. Later in his book he emphasised this turnaround by using St Paul's talk of 'laying off of the old man and putting on of the new'.[10]

It is all the more surprising that Kant said this as Kant subordinated theology to philosophy — the Biblical text has to be read in the light of the Kantian moral and rational approach. Kant was quite insistent that religious understanding must be subservient to moral and rational thought — except in the case of moral regeneration. Kant's appeal at this point to traditional Christian language of grace and divine aid means that there is a contradiction at the heart of his thought. He clearly considered that his own highly rational approach, which made God irrelevant except to guarantee the moral balance of the universe, does not succeed. In fact, there seems to be the implication that the effects of radical evil can only be broken by a specific historical occurrence, that is, the coming of Christ. Kant considers there is an intrinsic connection between the figure of Christ and what he called the 'breaking' of the power of radical evil which holds human beings.[11] Apparently if it were not for Jesus's existence, the power of evil would hold human beings fast. In all Kant's thought, history is subordinated to rationality but in this key area history appears to be decisive.

Kant, therefore, made a number of points:

1. There is a real, noumenal world but this world as it is in itself, independent of the way we perceive it, is unknowable.
2. The world which we know, the world in which science holds sway, is the phenomenal world, the world as we experience it. (Kant was a realist and firmly supported science which can give us real knowledge of the world as it is experienced.)
3. God exists, but God's existence cannot be proved in the way that the claims of science can.
4. Human beings are free, autonomous and rational, but they can place themselves into bondage to evil.
5. This bondage comes about when the underlying maxims of human actions become radically evil. Once this happens, only an act of God can release a person from bondage.

Although Kant rejected metaphysics, he still retained the idea of the noumenal world and God as guarantors of our knowledge of the phenomenal world. However, he opened up a divide between the phenomenal world and the real world that led to the scepticism that is so persistent today.

Kant brought together rationality and science, and a firm belief in God and God's activity. However, he did not resolve the conflict between these two positions and his work marked the beginning of a divide in the road which still affects us. It is this divide between the two paths that lay open that interests me in this book. I will argue that most of philosophy has taken one path but that there is another alternative. First, however, it is important to consider two other figures: Hegel and Marx.

8

HEGEL AND MARX

After Kant, two pathways lay open:

1. To reject all ideas of God and a real world as traditionally conceived. This rejection left no underpinning for human knowledge of the world and, therefore, all that remained was knowledge that we construct.
2. To affirm the idea of God who is ontologically independent of the universe God created while nevertheless being immanent with it; and to affirm the idea of a real world which our claims to knowledge seek to approximate.

GEORG HEGEL

Hegel (1770–1831), one of the greatest successors to Kant, marked the beginning of a path that took the first of these two ideas seriously. Hegel rejected all ideas of a real world independent of the one we know. Hegel's philosophy, in turn, lead to Karl Marx and to complete rejection of God.

Hegel had gone a long way down this path, because for Hegel, God, Geist or Absolute Spirit was not an existing reality, ontologically independent of the universe and on which the universe depended. Instead, Geist was emerging into consciousness through human reason. Geist would only come to self-fulfilment at the end of history. The whole of history can be seen as the journey towards the self-realisation of Geist. This process accelerates with human beings coming to self-consciousness, as it is through human rationality that Geist emerges. Geist can be considered as the Absolute Spirit, the ultimate essence of existence. It is not the God of traditional Christianity, but is closer to a form of pantheism in which some form of developing spiritual reality is emerging.

This idea was, a long time later, to influence Teilhard de Chardin's attempt to bring history, science and theology together in an underlying spiritual reality. According to de Chardin, human and world evolution will be fulfilled in a final 'omega-point' of history, which is close to Hegel's view.

Hegel's position is not clear. He may be seen as either a realist or an anti-realist:

- He may be seen as a realist as he maintains that there is a real world, the world which we experience, and in which historical forces operate to bring Geist into self-realisation.
- He may be seen as an anti-realist as he rejects Aristotle's principle of non-contradiction, which is the single most important part of a realist position. Bivalence (the claim that statements are either true or false) rests on this.

Hegel's rejection of the principle of non-contradiction had far reaching consequences. It amounts to the rejection of the view that statements are either true or false. Hegel held that it is out of the conflict between contradictory positions that new insights and progress become possible. While Aristotle thought that the principle of contradiction marked the bounds of sense, for Hegel it was through apparent contradictions that the universe is led to completion and higher states of being emerge. Truth is found through paradoxes and the paradoxes are continually revolved through higher level of understanding.

The German nation and the German intellectual tradition represented, for Hegel, the pinnacle of human achievement and the most advanced stage of the development towards Geist. Many modern critics of Hegel see his emphasis on the supremacy of Western culture as one of his greatest weaknesses. And, as we shall see, postmodernism rejects any priority given to any single culture, and it rejects any preference for Western intellectualism over, say, Aboriginal spiritual insights.

It is widely accepted that, for Hegel, Geist emerged through history (Hegel was the first to write a philosophy of history) through the operation of the dialectical process whereby:

1. one view is put forward representing a *thesis*,
2. a counter view is proposed presenting an *anti-thesis*, and
3. out of the tension between these two positions a new and higher level insight emerges which forms a *synthesis*.

This, in turn, becomes a new *thesis* which is then opposed by a new *anti-thesis*, which in turn gives rise to a new *synthesis*, and so the process continues throughout history. In fact, Hegel never actually referred to thesis, antithesis and synthesis, although his predecessor Johann Fichte certainly did. However, Hegel held to the centrality of the dialectical process by which seeming opposites or contradictories are overcome in a historical process by reference to new and higher level insights.

Plato dismissed the world of experience and held that the world of the timeless and spaceless forms represent true reality. Kant held the noumenal world, the world as it really is, to be inaccessible. Hegel, by contrast, insisted that the everyday world of normal experience is the world in which Geist comes to self-realisation. He had, therefore, a far more positive view of the ordinary world than many preceding philosophers. This marked an important switch in this path from Kant.

Kant proposed that there are two worlds whereas Hegel proposed that there is only one. Thereafter any idea of an alternative, real world becomes unimportant, marking one of the most significant switches on this pathway. Human beings now become the place in which God's reality is unfolded and where God is to be found. God as traditionally defined has disappeared and even the pale God of Kant is now not needed. 'God' is now a label for the insights of rationality which emerge in human beings. Instead of theology, Hegel pointed to the understanding of history as the place where meaning, reason and value are to be found.

This switch away from an 'other-worldly' approach to one entirely concerned with everyday experience is one that is still reflected in the work of many modern theologians. Many of these people have ceased to emphasise any idea of a life after death or the experience of God. Instead God is experienced in the day-to-day reality of the world, and nowhere else.[1]

Hegel affirmed Christianity, at least Christianity as it was understood through his philosophical system. He saw Christ bringing together God and humankind, effectively resolving the dialectical tension between the two poles. Hegel considered the Holy Spirit to be of central importance as it affirmed the idea of Geist which emerges to self-consciousness in history. He therefore continued to use traditional Christian terminology, but redeployed and redefined. This is a feature of many modern theologians today.

For Hegel, religious claims such as those made by Christianity were to a certain extent true, but certainly not absolutely true. They represented a stage in the gradual emergence of the absolute idea and, for Hegel, philosophy was supreme above theology. He had a highly optimistic view of the use of reason and the developing understanding of the world. Hegel's philosophy was to lead directly to Marx.

KARL MARX

Marx (1818–1883) was to take the divide in the philosophic pathway which began after Kant much further than Hegel. He rejected Hegel's claims to a spiritual side of the development of human history maintaining that all that mattered was the material and human life in the material world. Marx, thus, placed more emphasis on a this-worldly approach to reality.

Marx rejected religion as 'the opium of the masses'. He saw religion as the means by which the mass of ordinary, working people were kept in a state of subjugation and acceptance of their lot while the capitalists and land owners prospered from ordinary people's labour. Marx saw the churches as a means of social control to keep ordinary people in order. Today, for example, he would look at the role of the Catholic Church in, say, South America, the way it is orientated towards the wealthy (with the honourable exception of such people as the Jesuits and some other religious orders which work with the poor and the marginalised) and the maintenance of the status quo as a justification for his position. He emphasised the inevitability of the class struggle leading to a human utopia which would necessarily evolve through history. If human beings had to suffer as a means to this final end, then this was a worthwhile price to pay.

Marx saw himself engaged in sketching a noble human endeavour which was for the good of the masses. One of his famous quotations asserts that 'Philosophers have only interpreted the world in various ways; the task is to change it'. He lived most of his life in poverty and was completely committed to the truth of the ideas for which he stood. He saw the privileged class as being evil and self-interested, intent on maintaining their privileged position which, he considered, was dependent on the labour of neglected workers. His concern was to bring about change, to literally revolutionise society. It is, perhaps, not surprising that so many intelligent, sensitive and dedicated individuals have been inspired by the vision Marx presented and by the communist system to which it gave rise. It is significant, however, that the nearest human beings have ever come to a true community was in the early Christian Church where 'all things were held in common'[2] or in a monastery or convent. In all other arenas the practical outworkings of Marx's ideal have, so far, been a disappointment, despite some positive examples such as in Cuba where the level of education and social care have been admirable.

For Marx, who also used Hegel's dialectical approach to history and who acknowledged the influence of Hegel, there was an historical inevitability in the decline of capitalism and the rise of communism. Class struggle was an inevitable part of the dialectical process and the final outcome was assured. The proletariat was 'the class that holds the future in its hands'. He devoted most of his life to the study of capitalism and economics but, as with Hegel, it was the pressure of historical forces that led him to be so sure of the eventual victory of the working people.

God had no place within Marx's system. Marx restricted his observations to consideration of human material motivations since there was nothing else but the human arena.

Both Hegel and Marx, then, were optimists but their optimism was confined entirely to this life. While Hegel at least recognised an eventual omega point and saw value in his understanding of talk about God, Marx moved considerably beyond him in asserting the negative value of all such theological language.

Marx' influence today has waned with the collapse of communism, but the influence of his contemporary, Nietzsche, is today more profound even though this influence is not always recognised.

9

NIETZSCHE AND IVAN KARAMAZOV

FRIEDRICH NIETZSCHE

Nietzsche (1844–1900) was born on 15 October 1844 to devout Lutheran parents. While he was an implacable foe of Christianity, he nevertheless always discouraged convinced Christians from reading his books. When Nietzsche was composing *Thus Spake Zarathustra*, a young lady asked if he had been to church that day, to which he replied: 'Today, no.' He said afterwards to a friend: 'If I had troubled that girl's mind I should have been horrified.'

In a letter to his sister, who was a believing Christian, he wrote:

> ... What is it we are seeking? Rest and Happiness? No, nothing but Truth, however evil and terrible it may be ... So are the ways of men marked out; if you desire peace of soul and happiness, believe; if you would become a disciple of Truth, enquire ...[1]

This book is about *truth*, and from this quotation it would seem that Nietzsche might have approved of this enterprise. As a philosopher, I hope he would have done so, but the conclusion towards which this book is arguing is going to be radically different from his although I share with him a passionate commitment to the importance of truth.

Probably the largest single influence on Nietzsche was the work of Arthur Schopenhauer, whose gloomy, atheistic approach to life appealed to him strongly. In terms of outlook, however, Nietzsche was a much more life affirming, positive, sometimes laughing and even joyous figure than Schopenhauer.[2] Nietzsche himself said that it was Schopenhauer's atheism that was the prime attraction to him.[3] Schopenhauer rejected not only God but also metaphysics and any idea of the transcendent or the supernatural. He was, therefore, very different from Kant. Schopenhauer maintained that the universe was fundamentally irrational. He thus provided a marked contrast to the far more popular Hegel who saw meaning and value in the universe, a position which both Schopenhauer and Nietzsche totally rejected.

In *Thus Spake Zarathustra* Nietzsche wrote about the influence of Schopenhauer and his denial of life. Nietzsche was not a pessimist, however, calling people to deny life in the face of its meaninglessness. Instead, he called on people to live life to the full. Put crudely, Schopenhauer was an atheist, a pessimist and someone who did not engage with the world. He was someone who effectively denied life and said 'no' to it. By contrast Nietzsche was an atheist but an optimist and an activist in the world. He wished those who accepted his position to give a resounding 'yes' to life.

Nietzsche is famous for his proclamation that 'God is dead', a claim that needs to be properly understood. Nietzsche did not reject the God of traditional Christianity, Islam and Judaism in the way that an atheist might. Instead he rejected a way of looking at the world and the possibility of a God's eye view, of some absolute perspective from which the world can be viewed. With the death of God goes the death of all the Platonic and absolute values. God dies, and so do metaphysics, truth, goodness, justice and virtue. The goal of seeking some absolute truth is, according to Nietzsche, as dead and as futile as God. This is of extreme importance. With the rejection of God goes the rejection of everything with which the word God is traditionally associated, including all absolutes.

What, then, is truth? According to Nietzsche it is:

> A mobile army of metaphors, metonyms, anthropomorphisms: in short a sum of human relations which become poetically and rhetorically intensified, metamorphosed, adorned and after a long usage seem to a nation fixed, canonic, binding; truths are illusions of which one has forgotten that they are illusions.[4]

A human being does not discover truths. Rather, he or she '... always discovered in things only that which he had put into them!'[5]

According to Nietzsche, morality itself is a sign of decadence[6] because it is holding onto the view that there are such things as values, virtues and good and evil. No such things exist, according to Nietzsche, except in so far as human beings are held to have created them. 'God is dead' because God is now recognised as something humans have created and, with this recognition, all those things which the word 'God' stood for (such as absolute value and truth) die as well.

We have seen that, prior to Kant, God underpinned knowledge of the real world. Nietzsche represents the culmination of the path which denies God and with God dies any idea of truth, value or knowledge of the world itself. His eventual idea of the summit of human development, the superman, moves beyond good and evil — categories that no longer have meaning.

Nietzsche's work, if accepted, marks the end of an era of metaphysical enquiries and the logical culmination of one of the paths stemming from Kant. God, and with God any real noumenal world, has gone and with them all meaning, morality and metaphysics. There is no ready-made world which we discover, no essential nature of a thing as Aristotle thought, and there is only our own perspective.[7] Human beings are on their own with no landmarks to guide them in a sea of relativity. They can now become gods if they will throw off the trappings of convention which seek to shackle and constrain them with now discredited modes of thinking. Christianity is rejected because Nietzsche considered it to be a religion of self-denial which undermines the humanity of people.

Nietzsche did not consider that life had any aim or point, but he considered that exceptional human beings have to come to the state where they can give life a purpose or aim. For Nietzsche, the highest human aim is to achieve the status of the superman — the person valid by his own will alone, free from the constants of conventional morality. This is an almost evolutionary step for individual human beings, moving beyond the herd of humanity to the evolution of a new and higher level man. This is, of course, a highly elitist view and the common herd of human beings is needed as a means to the end of the emergence of the higher individual.

Effectively, Nietzsche considered slavery to be the basis of culture, and it is out of slavery that the higher individual can emerge. In *The Dawn of Day*, Nietzsche admitted that some will have to do the boring, rough and dirty work of society in order that the higher level individuals may emerge. There is truth in this. The brilliance of Greek philosophy or Renaissance art was possible partly because of the leisure afforded to a narrow range of people by the work of slaves. The great art of the Middle Ages was possible only because of the labour and suffering of untold thousands who worked to create the wealth and to build the cathedrals that enabled the art to be created.

There is an even worse enemy than the herd to the strong individual who affirms life in a positive way. This is Christianity. Christianity and its morality, Nietzsche claimed, act like leeches which destroy the affirmation of life held by the strong man.

It was Christianity, above all else, that destroyed the achievements and the might of Rome:

> Christianity was the vampire of the imperium Romanum — in a night it shattered the tremendous achievement of the Romans.[8]

The Roman Empire was, according to Nietzsche, the most tremendous achievement of human organisation. The Romans had instinctive nobility and taste, tremendous style and art, and a willingness to say 'Yes!' to life. Yet, Christianity destroyed the Roman Empire until:

> ... no two stones were left standing one on the other — until even the Teutons and other clodhoppers were able to become master of it.[9]

The Romans were triumphant over the whole known world. For many centuries, nothing could stand against them until, in Nietzsche's view, they were conquered from within by the insidious disease of Christianity which sapped the energy of a mighty empire. The Roman Empire was not:

> ... stamped to death by Teutons and other heavy-footed vandals! But destroyed by crafty, stealthy, invisible, anaemic vampires! Not conquered, but only drained of blood! ... Everything wretched inwardly ailing, and full of ignoble feelings, the whole Ghetto-world of souls was in a trice uppermost! ... they [Christians] are not even men. If Islam despises Christianity, it is justified a thousand times over; for Islam presupposes men.[10]

Nietzsche considered that Christianity is a denial of life. It made human beings sick from within. The Church deliberately ruined people by making them weak, and it did this by claiming to 'improve' them. It was not only in Roman times that Christianity enfeebled the noble spirit, it did the same in the Middle Ages when the Church destroyed the 'noble Germans' under the excuse of 'improving' them, leaving them as:

> ... a caricature of man, like an abortion: he had become a 'sinner', he was caged up, he had been imprisoned behind a host of appalling notions ... full of hate for the instincts of life, full of suspicion in regard to all that is still strong and happy. In short, a 'Christian'.[11]

The Christian commits the fundamental crime against life by preaching all that weakens and enfeebles in place of those things which ennoble and strengthen. The Christian concept of God is a God who denies life and therefore destroys human beings from within. Morality is the enemy of the true, noble human nature:

> All ancient moral-mongers were unanimous on this point, 'it is necessary to kill passion'.[12]

The Church attacked passion (St Augustine is a good example of this),[13] and in so doing attacked life itself and the will to power. God, naturally, underpins Christianity and Christianity is false because 'God is dead'. The very idea of God is, according to Nietzsche, hostile to life and with the death of God humans can become free of the God-chains they have constructed for themselves. Indeed, Nietzsche saw the human realisation of the death of God as an occasion for rejoicing, of liberation. Horizons were now opened which were previously closed. The God of Christianity is miserable:

> ... a hybrid creature of decay, nonentity, concept and contradiction, in which all the instincts of decadence, all the cowardices and langours of the soul find their sanction.[14]

It is not just the God of Christianity that Nietzsche wished to destroy, but the very ideal of what it is to be human that Christianity stands for. In the first volume of *Will to Power*, Nietzsche called for the destruction of this idea. The idea of a humble, compassionate, forgiving and charitable individual must be rejected and eliminated. Nietzsche called for lust, anger and revenge to be regarded as virtues rather than vices, for these were the marks of the strong person, while the Christian virtues were those of the weak.

This may seem surprising and unsettling, but with the death of God, as Nietzsche saw it, the logic of his position is apparent. At least this is an honest, clear and open position. It may be accepted or rejected, but the passion of Nietzsche's claim and the coherence of his position rightly places him as one of the most significant figures of the twentieth century. This is not the same as saying that his views are right, however.

Given the enormous influence that Nietzsche has had, it is important to recognise that he never actually proved any of his claims. What is more, he did not really argue his case. Rather, he made assertions and expected his readers to agree with him. In this sense he was more of a poet than a philosopher. To claim that 'the world has no meaning', which was a key starting point for Nietzsche, is in itself a truth claim about ultimate reality. As an example of Nietzsche's use of assertion as a tactic, he had, or at least seemed to have, based on some of his comments little regard for women. For instance, 'Man shall be trained for war, and women for the recreation of the warrior. All else is folly.'[15] Few modern thinkers would accept Nietzsche's opinion on this role of women, yet his claim that the world is meaningless is, also, little more than a statement of opinion. Of course he may be right; but, then, he may not be.

Nietzsche did have a clear view of what humans should become. He was not a relativist; he saw 'ordinary' human beings representing the means to the end of the 'higher', evolved being, the superman. Yet talk of what 'should be' or of something 'higher' is the reverse of meaninglessness. It is to have a view of what the universe is about and how human beings should respond. If the universe was truly meaningless, then any response would be as good as any other. Nietzsche clearly does not consider this to be the case.

Nietzsche's appeal is that of a visionary, and there is no compelling reason why his analysis of the human condition or the nature of reality should be accepted, yet it has had a crucial influence on the development of post-modernism. Nietzsche himself disliked people and loved animals, and he was declared clinically insane. While this, in itself, does not invalidate his ideas, one should at least take a pause before accepting his views.

Kant placed the noumenal world beyond human access but retained a role for God. Hegel and Marx remained optimistic about the world and effectively rejected the traditional idea of God. Nietzsche went further to abandon God entirely and with God any idea of metaphysics and of truth. Yet he still, in spite of himself, was not a relativist. Many twentieth century philosophers have taken the divide after Kant much further than Nietzsche. Sartre rejected the idea of a common human anthropology, maintaining that human beings have the ability to choose what to become. Personal authenticity in this choice is the highest value.[16] This process has continued still further, elaborating and developing the path from Kant. Before examining more these recent developments, however, one other figure who stands at the beginning of the present age needs to be considered. That is a literary creation, Dostoyevsky's Ivan Karamazov.

IVAN KARAMAZOV

Dostoyevsky's *The Brothers Karamazov* is a novel about three brothers, Ivan, Dimitri and Alyosha, but it is the fictional confrontation between two of them, Ivan and Alyosha, that has had most influence. Ivan Karamazov is the worldly wise young man who has been to the big city and has returned to his father's home after an absence of some years. He and Alyosha meet and get acquainted once again. Ivan knows that Alyosha believes in God and has joined the local monastery. He says that he also believes in God, but he cannot accept the world God made and therefore cannot accept God as the creator of this world. Ivan cannot accept God because of the suffering of innocent children. He then proceeds to tell three stories (which we now know were taken from Russian newspapers at the time).

In the first story a little girl wets her bed one night. Her mother strips her naked, covers her with her own excrement and makes her eat it, and then locks her all night in a little outside toilet where she beats with her tiny fists on the door praying to her 'dear kind God'. Ivan says that nothing, no eventual end, is worth the tears of this child.

The second story is about a boy who throws a stone and hurts the leg of one of the local lord's dogs. When the lord next goes out hunting, he notices that his favourite dog is limping, and he finds out why. He calls the boy and his parents, and has the boy stripped and then sets him off running across the fields. He then sets the hounds onto him and they tear him to pieces. Ivan asks Alyosha what he would do with this lord. In a small voice, Alyosha replies, 'Shoot him.' 'Bravo!' says Ivan, 'You're a fine hermit!' In other words, even the monk Alyosha is appalled. Ivan admits that at the end of time the boy, his parents and the lord may all embrace and shout 'Hosanna', but he cannot accept this. Nothing, he claims is worth the suffering of this boy and no eventual end can justify it.

The third story is about the time when southern Russia was invaded by Turks, who, Ivan says, love children. Ivan quotes to Alyosha examples where the Turks took the babies of Russian mothers and got them to smile up at them, tickling them under their chins. They then shot them through the eyes. The fun was doing it in front of the mothers.

Ivan says that, in his view, NOTHING is worth the suffering of innocent children, and no eventual end for the world can justify their suffering. Ivan admits that adults suffer, but concedes that in some way they may be responsible for their own suffering. He claims that whatever God's purposes in creating the universe may be, if the suffering of innocent children is the price that has to be paid, then it is not worth it. Ivan rejects the God who allows such suffering. Ivan also rejects any appeal to human freedom making human beings responsible because God is omniscient. God KNEW what human beings would do with their freedom, yet he created the world in which these things would happen. God, therefore, cannot be absolved from responsibility.

We do not need to look to fiction for examples of suffering, for we have real-life examples in plenty, including Port Arthur in Tasmania, Bosnia, Kosovo, Rwanda, Pol Pot's regime in Cambodia and the Holocaust. Ivan Karamazov would have stood by the lime pits in Belsen and Auschwitz and, while believing that God exists, would have rejected God because nothing could justify the suffering of the innocent children who died there. Ivan would have taken a similar position if he had watched Hutu villagers chop of the arms and legs off their Tutsi neighbours' children leaving them to bleed to death in front of their parents. He would have had the same response while watching Pol Pot's soldiers pile the bodies of hundreds of children of middle-class Cambodians on top of each other before they were burnt.

Elie Weisel, a Holocaust survivor, gives an account of the Holocaust. In his book *The Night* there are far worse accounts of suffering than those described by Ivan, as here the State and modern technology have brought suffering down to a fine art. For Weisel, like Ivan, it is the suffering of children that leads him to abandon belief in God:

> Never shall I forget that night, the first night in camp, which has turned my life into one long night, seven times cursed and seven times sealed. Never shall I forget that smoke. Never shall I forget the little faces of the children, whose bodies turned into wreaths of smoke beneath a silent blue sky. Never shall I forget those flames which consumed my faith forever. Never shall I forget that nocturnal silence which deprived me, for all eternity, of the desire to live. Never shall I forget those moments which murdered my God and my soul and turned my dreams into dust. Never shall I forget these things, even if I am condemned to live as long as God Himself. Never.[17]

Weisel echoes Ivan's words in a conversation with his father the first time he saw a lorry load of dead babies being consigned to the incinerator:

> 'I could not believe that they could burn people of our age, that humanity would ever tolerate it.'

> His father replies, 'Humanity? Humanity is not concerned with us. Today anything is allowed.'[18]

Notice how '... anything is allowed' echoes Nietzsche's position that with the death of God, all values disappear as well. In the Nuremberg war crimes trial, a former Polish guard at Auschwitz describes how children were thrown straight into the furnaces without first being gassed. He said:

> They threw them in alive. Their screams could be heard at the camp. We don't know whether they wanted to economise on gas, or if it was because there was not enough room in the gas chambers.[19]

Albert Camus' novels *The Plague* and *The Night* are his attempt to wrestle with what happened to the rebellion against God, because, within seventy years, a rebellion against God that started in the name of humanity led to Stalin and Hitler's death camps. In *The Plague* the Jesuit priest and the doctor clash over the plague. The priest sees it as being sent by God because of the sin of the people and the doctor rejects this, and fights the plague with all his energy. They come to a sort of unity after staying up all night fighting unsuccessfully for a child who dies in great pain and the priest is no longer able to see the plague as a punishment brought by God. Retaining faith in the presence of extreme innocent suffering is not easy.

Ivan places human justice above God and the result, seemingly, is the Holocaust. With the rebellion against God came the desire to maintain the divinity of man, but as Ivan Karamazov says, once God is rejected, then 'everything is permitted' because all norms of conduct, all virtue and all meaning disappear as well. In this sense, then, Ivan Karamazov and Nietzsche are intellectual allies, they even share similarities of character and disposition, and both ended by being effectively mad.

The coupling of the philosopher Nietzsche with the fictional Ivan Karamazov seems unlikely but they are seminal figures in a path away from God that leads to meaninglessness. They are not, however, the only ones on this path.

THE DENIAL OF
A REAL WORLD

Many modern philosophers wish to dismiss all talk of a Kantian 'thing in itself', of a world independent of what we perceive. In throwing out Kant's noumenal world they, naturally, also throw out God and the idea of faith. Their arguments for rejecting such a world are not always convincing and often appear to owe more to an intuition that such a world is irrelevant to our knowledge claims than to any sustained attempt to argue that there is no such world. Some philosophers seem to dismiss any discussion of a 'world in itself'.

WILLARD VAN ORMAN QUINE

Quine (b. 1908) took a radical approach in that he rejected all ontological talk — or at least he redefined it so that it is completely different from the idea of ontology (see p. 66). By 'ontological talk' Quine meant merely what a particular theory says exists. Normally one would consider that talk of ontology (what there is) is prior to talk of epistemology (how we can know what there is), but this is not the case for Quine. He considered that epistemology gives rise to ontology, that is, what there is depends on what we say there is within a particular theory

Quine rejected any talk of things existing or any search for what really exists, regarding it as a 'forlorn cause'.[1] Quine was totally uninterested in what really exists, for his interest was only in what exists within a given theory. In fact he went so far as to specifically claim that he was talking about epistemology and not metaphysics.[2] Quine's lack of interest in metaphysics is obvious, perhaps because he regarded it, as so many modern philosophers do, as an enterprise that Kant has shown to be folly. However, he did not take account of the importance Kant attached to the noumenal world or the religious faith to which it gave rise. It is perhaps significant that Quine did not argue why metaphysical and ontological questions — questions about the ultimate nature of reality — should not be of interest and should not be pursued. While Kant considered there was a real 'world in itself' even though this was inaccessible to us, Quine simply showed no interest in the possibility of such a world. The furthest that Quine went in being interested in ontology is to consider what exists within a given theory.

For Quine, human beings impose a conceptual scheme, a fabric which they create. As Sachs' put it:

> And, with regard to their status with a theory, physical objects and Homer's gods are indeed identical ... The further issue of what is real, in the sense defined above, that is, what exists independently of all experience, is not one that Quine is, or considers that he should be, interested in at all ... Quine understands ontological talk as describing the objects into which a given theory slices reality; the concern is the ontological commitment within a theory.[3]

This raises a question: If human beings impose a fabric, then on what is the fabric imposed? Unless Quine was an ontological idealist and maintained that the physical world is mind-dependent, then surely there must be some real world on which, on Quine's view, human beings impose a fabric which they construe as ultimate reality? In fact, Quine did at some stages actually refer to human beings imposing order on reality.[4] This is a major concession because if there is some reality on which we impose a fabric, a cloak of interpretation, then it leaves the clear implication that there exists a reality on which we impose and this reality must shape what we see. Imagine putting a sheet over some objects. If all we can see is the sheet, we may nevertheless have to accept that the sheet is affected by the objects beneath it. If the sheet is the order we impose, it does not follow that there is not a reality beneath it about which we should be concerned. Quine was content to ignore this reality altogether.

PETER STRAWSON

Strawson, in his early days, rejected the correspondence theory of truth and maintained that to say that a statement is true, does not add anything to the statement; it merely endorses the statement. Thus, 'This is a good torch' says no less than 'It is true that this is a good torch'. All the second statement does is to show our support for the first statement. When we say that a statement 'is true', all we are doing is confirming or endorsing the statement. In saying this, Strawson was drawing on the work of G.E. Moore who said that 'good' was a non-natural property. When a thing has a property called being 'good' then this property cannot be analysed any further.

R.M. Hare rejected the idea that in calling something good we are ascribing a property to it. All we are doing, Hare maintained, is commending or praising the thing in question. The early Strawson maintained that 'true' works like Hare's use of 'good'; to say a statement is true is merely an extension of this. To say 'It is true that the snow is white' is simply commending or confirming the statement 'The snow is white'.

It is not surprising that, given this view, Strawson rejected Kant's understanding of a world-in-itself. Kant argued for 'ontological realism', which maintains that there is a real world but that we cannot know what this world is like (see chapter 7). Kant's answer to the question 'How can we know the world is as we experience it?' is that we cannot know. All that we know is the world as we experience it and we can be certain about such knowledge, but this is not knowledge about the real world.

Strawson, in his book *The Bounds of Sense*[5] rejected Kant's talk of a noumenal world as unintelligible. He wanted no involvement with talk of what is real independent of the way it is experienced by us. Strawson wished to explore the structures of our thought about the world. He wanted to maintain that what is real is what we experience and there is no world beyond this (knowable or otherwise) which need in any way concern us. However, this presented Strawson with a real problem. Unless:

1. he said, with Berkeley and the idealists, that the world is the creation of our minds (and he did not do this) then
2. he had to admit the possibility of there being a real world independent of the way we experience it, and if he made this (Kantian) assumption; then

3. he also had the Kantian problem of not being sure that what we experience is as it really is.

The only way of being totally sure that our knowledge of the world is of the world as it REALLY is rather than as we experience it, is if we create the world. We can then claim certainty about our knowledge since our knowledge is of what we have created. If this is not the case, then philosophers will always be plagued with the question, 'How do we KNOW that what we take as true is true?'. Strawson wants to reject all such metaphysical questions and sees them as irrelevant. They cannot be irrelevant, however, as long as one grants that the world is real and not a projection of human minds. If there is a real world, we will always be, or at least some of us will always be, tormented by the age-old epistemological worry about whether what we know is true.

Richard Rorty rejected all attempts to provide foundations for knowledge and maintained that philosophers have 'talked themselves out of a job'. In particular they have not had regard to the workings of history. In 'The world well lost', Rorty rejected the notion of a real, independently existing world beyond all conceptual schemes, asserting:

> I think that the realistic true believer's notion of the world is an obsession rather than an intuition.[6]

This is a major claim and you would expect it to be supported by detailed argument, but it is not. Certainly realists will be obsessed by the notion of a real world and in this sense will be 'true believers', a term which Rorty clearly intended to use in a mocking tone. Realists may even be prepared to admit that their concern is indeed an obsession, but will claim that it is a very reasonable one given that no philosophic argument has been produced to show that there is no real world. In fact, Rorty admitted his lack of argument:

> I have no argument against the true believer's description of our so-called 'intuitions'. All that can be done with the claim that 'only the world determines truth' is to point out the equivocation in the realist's use of 'world'.[7]

For Rorty, truth is 'What our peers will let us get away with saying',[8] and there is no truth beyond this. Rorty is essentially a pragmatist, almost in the tradition of William James. He sees truth as what is agreed among a community of those who are like-minded and any attempt to get behind this to some absolute truth he sees as being folly.

The problem is that if this view is accepted, truth becomes relative to different communities and resides in majority opinion. Rorty does not seem to acknowledge this but, effectively, he is appealing to people who, like him, inhabit a Western, democratic world which has its roots in Greek philosophy and who would see any alternative as something to dismiss with incredulity. However incredulity is not a substitute for argument.

It is as if the sceptic about God, an absolute morality or any independent standard of aesthetics reject all talk of God, morality and aesthetics but do so by simply saying that those who use such talk are only expressing their own views. We have here clear echoes of the anti-realist approach set out in the previous chapter, in other words echoes of the idea that truth is relative to the framework within which one operates. Any idea of some absolute reality is dismissed as effectively an obsession and those who hold such views are made to feel naive and inadequate.

The trouble is when majority academic opinion comes together it becomes a very effective vehicle for marginalising any alternatives. British, American, Canadian, Australian and New Zealand academic philosophers contribute to the same academic journals, apply for jobs in the same institutions, cite each other's work and attend the same conferences. Through this process there builds up an accepted view of what philosophy is about. An orthodoxy is constructed and one will only get an academic job if one plays the game of the orthodox and accepts their presuppositions. If truth is considered to be the majority view, then the majority can be highly effective at marginalising the minority and less fashionable views. However, the majority view is not necessarily right.

The emphasis in the modern academic world is on publication in 'refereed journals' (academic journals where the editor consults academic referees before deciding what is to be published). Contributions to these journals are an important way of determining the 'research rating' for a university department or institution and this, in turn, determines the funds that institution will receive. This practice tends to accentuate the 'industry' of academics writing for the sake of writing and producing material that is chiefly of interest to other academics rather than engaging in the wider world and its interests. In Britain, institutions will actually seek to 'buy in' staff with a good 'research output' (measured in terms of publications in refereed journals) as this will positively effect the funding they receive from the government. A modern-day Wittgenstein who hardly wrote anything and who certainly wrote no journal articles would probably find it exceedingly difficult to obtain employment.

Anglo-American analytic philosophy now has little interest in questions of God or the real world, little interest in any search or understanding of any claim to ultimate Truth. This is understandable, but this is not the same as saying that it is acceptable or that it represents a truthful representation of the most important questions facing human beings.

The denial of a real world, therefore, although now widely accepted by many philosophers, still faces a challenge. If there is a real world, it will constantly challenge our claims to truth because whatever we think we know lies beyond the frontiers of our mapping. If there is, indeed, no real world, then post-modernism provides a logical way forward, and it is to this that we now turn.

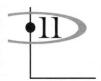

POST-MODERNISM

There is no clear point in time when post-modernism began, nor is there a clear definition of what it is. In fact there is no single position which is 'the' post-modern position, as it covers a range of different responses to the modern world.

The term 'post-modernism' was first used in the late 1930s by the English historian Arnold Toynbee. It is a particular phenomenon of French culture. French philosophy, which is very different from Anglo-American, lays particular stress on the French language and the power of texts, which is clearly in evidence in post-modernism. Post-modernism may be connected with the student riots in Paris in 1968 and the Marxism and anarchist sentiments that lay beneath French culture at the time.

To the post-modern mind, context and perspective are everything. There is more than one form of post-modernism, but at least in some versions the reality we talk about and inhabit is one that we construct, that can be radically altered and one that has no fixed points of reference. In post-modernism there is no good or bad art, only the appreciation and interpretation each individual brings to what he or she sees. Thus, a painting using elephant dung that won the Turner Prize for art in Britain, a pile of bricks that was exhibited at the Tate Gallery and a sheep preserved in formaldehyde that was regarded as one of the great British modern works of art are all considered to rank equally with the paintings of Turner, Constable and Picasso.

It may be helpful to briefly discuss the distinction previously made between two positions, both of which are loosely, and perhaps inaccurately, described as 'post-modern'.

JACQUES DERRIDA AND EMMANUEL LEVINAS

On the one hand, there are Derrida, Levinas and those who have been influenced by them who do not accept the idea of meaning-lessness, and indeed affirm the central human responsibility to 'the other' and the centrality of justice. In fact, Levinas would probably object strongly to even being called a post-modernist and his passionate commitment to justice and to the 'other' may make him a philosophic realist.

Derrida claims that every reading of a text is as much a misinterpretation as it is an interpretation because all terms are devoid of meaning except the meaning constructed for them. The same applies to readings of history or appreciation of art.

Derrida should not, however, be seen as a radical relativist. In *The Force of Law*[1] he writes that 'deconstruction is justice'. It is an infinite demand to recognise what fails to be said and to recognise that our attempts to realise justice in our legal codes are necessarily imperfect. We simply cannot know enough about people to fulfil the real demand of justice. Law-making activity is necessary as an on-going process but it needs to be accompanied by a recognition of its inherent inadequacy. Similarly in his book *Spectres of Marx*,[2] Derrida maintains that Marxism went wrong in forgetting the Messianic vision and ideals that it had. Thus, for Derrida, to see texts as fixed and rigid is to fail to do justice to their very nature. Whatever our interpretation of any text (legal, historical, philosophic or religious), there is a 'more' which we cannot capture. Human beings have a duty to witness to this 'more', this 'otherness', in and through the language they use. Much of Derrida's language is poetic, a play on words. He uses this technique to draw attention to what is *not* being said, which he sees as more important than what *is* being said.

Derrida considers literature of crucial importance, but denies our ability to be able to arrive at any single correct interpretation of it. He emphasises the importance of the text itself and does not seek reference to any external world. Derrida's claim that 'there is nothing outside the text' is often misinterpreted to mean that 'anything goes', any interpretation will do. However, his concern is to challenge the assumption that words are firmly rooted to what they signify and to reject the possibility of an objective or neutral perspective.

Levinas is more of a realist than a post-modernist but he mistrusts philosophic justification of any realist position. For him, truth is grounded in the face of the absolute demand made on us by the 'other', the demand to which every human being is bound to respond. Levinas stands for ethical realism rather than ontological realism — he is not a relativist in the field of morality and sees an absolute demand of justice being made on each of us by the 'other' human being we confront. Truth, for Levinas, is embodied in humanity.

It is important, therefore, not to automatically equate post-modernism with relativism. Some post-modernists are relativists, but not all are.

THE NIETZSCHE STRAND OF POST-MODERNISM

Very different from Derrida and Levinas are philosophers such as Deleuze, Guattari, Baudrillard and Foucault who defend a position very close to that of Nietzsche and Rorty (see chapters 9 and 10). The Nietzschean strand of post-modernism is particularly critical of the Western, European cultural imposition which, it is held, is heavily based on a male, patriarchal, science and reason-based construction of reality. This legacy, which began with Plato and Aristotle, is seen as hierarchical, impoverishing and marginalising key elements of society. It imposes what 'should be' and reinforces the existing Western status quo based on reason and the enlightenment vision, based on Western philosophy and Western values. For post-modernism this is an artificial, alien and illegitimate imposition which, in particular, ignores the feminine perspective. There has been, therefore, a close link between post-modernism and much of modern feminist writings.

The Western elite, it is held, have imposed an agenda of their own which is brutalising and has resulted in great suffering. Marginal groups such as the poor, those with alternative cultures, colours, sexual orientations and all those who are in any way different find that these differences are oppressed and persecuted. This Western, patriarchal approach has been responsible for slavery, colonialism with the

suppression of indigenous societies and values,[3] as well as exploitation and the rape of the planet's resources.

It is held that there has been an imperialism in ideas and values,
coupled with an imperialism of culture and economics, designed to
entrench the values, world views and perspective of the Western elite.
What is more, this is given a cloak of respectability by a Western philosophical system which is in the service of those in power. Religion,
and Christianity in particular, has aided this exploitation by an imposition of thought forms, ideas, cultures and literature (including the
great works of Western literature such as the Bible, Shakespeare,
Dante, Milton, Tolstoy and Dostoyevsky[4]) which are alien to those on
which they are imposed. To the post-modern mind these represent no
more than one view among a myriad of others, none of which has any
claim to validity beyond its own perspective. In Western history,
whether in art, music, theology, philosophy or literature, the voice of
the feminine has been suppressed or marginalised in favour of male
values, which are oppressive and unjustifiable.

The attempt by Western society to impose a global hegemony,
by vehicles such as capitalism, the world bank, global satellite links,
advertising and a single world economic order, is precisely the sort
of exercise in dominance that post-modernism rejects. This is a
rejection of both the diversity and the emphasis on difference that
are post-modernism's central affirmations.

The same would, of course, be true for any non-Western system
(for instance Islam) which claimed that it had the 'right' answer and
which attempted to impose its beliefs. It is, perhaps, significant that
post-modernism shows its own hidden agenda by not attacking such
systems with anything like the attention or focus reserved for the
Western tradition. There are strong echoes of anarchism within
some strands of post-modernism which resists any authority and any
imposition of a system or rules. Nevertheless, by its own criteria,
post-modernism has its own authors, its own heroes and, more
commonly, heroines who are elevated to a status which, on their
own account, no-one should enjoy. Any philosophic, religious or
scientific framework needs to be abandoned or at least treated with
the gravest suspicion.

The very attempt to persuade another to one's own perspective
is an exercise in power. Nietzsche, as we have seen in chapter 9,
maintained that the use and abuse of power was a feature of all

humanity. Even those who sought to supposedly help others were thereby exercising a form of dominion over them. The will to power of one human being over another or of one society over another is endemic in the human condition and the 'superman' is the one who will refuse to be thus dominated and subjugated and who chooses his own path. Totalitarianism and power can be seen to go hand in hand.

Nietzsche is sometimes described as the philosopher of the German Nazis, but this is to totally misunderstand him. The Nazis developed an extreme, totalitarian system which Nietzsche would have rejected out of hand. When Nietzsche's madman in *The Gay Science* confronts the crowd in the market place and proclaims that 'God is dead ... We have killed him you and I', the madman goes on to ask:

> 'Is not the greatness of this deed too much for us? Must not we our-
> selves become gods simply to seem worthy of it? There has never
> been a greater deed — and whosoever shall be born after us, for the
> sake of this deed, shall be part of a great humanity than all history.'[5]

The death of God opens the way for the superman, the man who throws aside all the trappings of convention and imposed world views. As Feuerbach realised,[6] man has, in becoming the measure of all things, also become God, and Habermas sees Nietzsche as marking the advent of post-modernity.[7]

The French philosopher and social critic Michel Foucault (1926–1984) considered that truth, far from being something to applaud, was in fact used as a means of oppression. He rejected the very idea that some ideas are preferable to others because they are 'true' or 'more true' than others. Claims to truth represent a system of exclusion by which circles of power are maintained and developed. This is a relatively early expression of the view that post-modernism was later to expound in a more developed form.

This strand of post-modernism involves a rejection of any commitment to ontology or to any attempt to make sense of the world by means of seeking a truth about the world. It is not just that, as with Kant, there is a real world which is unknowable; to the post-modernist there is no ontological reality, no 'world-in-itself'. All human knowledge and reality itself is constructed by human beings and is therefore radically perspectival. Language is, as Wittgenstein put it, a 'cage' in which we are forever locked, and we are born into the cage that is the reality we experience unless we choose to move to a different cage. However, this reality is forever changing. Indeed, the one thing that is certain is that change is constant. There is no true meaning, whether for life, religion, morality or even a text, since the way that a text is interpreted will depend on the culture within which it is read. Post-modern critics and philosophers will happily explore and discuss the myriad perspectives represented by different human cages, but they will strongly resist any attempt to find the one true cage or any suggestion that one cage is to be preferred to another.

There are no absolutes, no rocks of certainty on which one can stand firm outside the constant sea of change. We are embedded in these tossing and raging waters and reality is merely our own perspective. The most we can achieve is to, by great effort, understand another's perspective while recognising that he or she is also immersed in the constant waters of change, but his or her perspective is no more privileged than ours. The search for certainty or for any rock to cling to is folly. Truth (at least with a capital 'T') has become a dirty word, a word used only by those who have failed to appreciate the human condition and who are embedded in a world view which is considered discredited. As Nietzsche put it, '... facts are precisely what there is not, only interpretations'.[8]

What may be regarded as the 'Nietzschean' strand of post-modernism rests on an underlying nihilism, but this may be more a feature of what might be termed 'post-modern culture' than representing particular philosophers in the post-modern tradition. It is not possible to fully analyse what the post-modern is; the ephemeral has pride of place. The search is an end in itself and the possibility of any ultimate or single truth is either denied or said to be unavailable. It is not possible to exhaust what the post-modern is because there is no firm definition, no way of capturing reality which cannot itself be challenged and broken down. The search is an end in itself and the possibility of truth is denied. Truth is always on the horizon and never to be immediately grasped or understood. Either the horizon is unattainable because there is nothing to attain or it is so radically perspectival that no single portrayal will capture it.

Once one has seen that the Earth goes round the Sun and that the Sun is a relatively unimportant planet in a minor galaxy, one will have little to say to a friend who still considers that the world is flat and that the Sun goes round the Earth. The perspectival shift is so great that communication becomes almost impossible, and the only hope may be to try to persuade the friend to open their minds and to see the situation in a new way. So it is with post-modernists and those they see as being still obsessed by the old ideas of metaphysics and a search for truth. They share a mutual incomprehension and, to the post-modernist, the friend needs to expand his or her vision, to come out of the trenches formed by his mind and to see the world in a broader perspective. Argument will not achieve the shift in perspective. What is needed is for the friend to stop closing his mind and to be open to new, and possibly threatening, possibilities, to be able to live on the sea of uncertainty with no fixed marks and where nothing abides or endures.

Even science is not immune from the radical relativity that this form of post-modernism proposes. Karl Popper and Thomas Kuhn in the field of philosophy of science argued that science does not produce knowledge that is probable or even certain. Kuhn's analysis of the history of science is challenging as he speaks of sudden paradigm shifts rather than science challenging its own ways of interpreting reality. He maintained that the scientific enterprise is conditioned to support existing paradigms. Results that might challenge existing paradigms tend to be suppressed or not investigated. The academic world itself supports this approach with the older generation controlling the funds and the power which young and more radical thinkers may have to conform to if they are to succeed. Sudden paradigm shifts take place so that scientists working within different paradigms may literally be working in different worlds and it may be almost impossible to communicate. The same happens in philosophy when Anglo-American analytic philosophers generally dismiss or find incomprehensible much of continental philosophy, and vice versa.

Karl Popper held that there were rational grounds for choosing one scientific paradigm rather than another, but Kuhn's analysis undermined this. Progress in science is not a development towards greater and greater understanding of a singe objective reality; it is not a closer and closer vision of 'the truth', rather the truth that science affirms is relative to the paradigm selected. Even in science, therefore, the idea of a single truth seems to be undermined.

For someone to claim that there is a 'post-modern view of the world' almost amounts to a contradiction, as the most that might be said is that there is no single view of the world. The post-modernist rejects any idea of good art, as of beauty and of truth. We are children of a sea of flux and, now that God has been rejected as an underpinning of beauty, art, culture and truth, there is no authenticity:

> The contemporary writer ... is forced to start from scratch: reality doesn't exist, time doesn't exist, personality doesn't exist. God was the omniscient author, but he died, now no-one knows the plot, and since our reality lacks the sanction of a creator, there's no guarantee as to the authenticity of the received version ...Time is no longer purposive ... and so there is only chance. Reality is, simply, our experience, and objectivity is, of course, an illusion. Personality, after passing through a stage of awkward self-consciousness, has become ... a mere locus for our experience. In view of these annihilations, it should be no surprise that literature, also, does not exist — how could it? There is only reading and writing ... ways of maintaining a considered boredom in the face of the abyss.[9]

The post-modern individual lives in a world of radical openness and uncertainty. This is liberating, and invigorating as there are no boundaries, nothing that cannot be challenged and can lead to great creativity. Human beings are seen as finite and insignificant, and we have to find the courage in ourselves (for there is nothing else) to be able to face this finitude and the radical uncertainty that accompanies it.

The idea that we have to create our own values seems to be supported by many scientists such as Richard Dawkins who claim that human beings are effectively mechanisms for our genes to replicate and to transmit themselves through the generations. We are organic mechanisms which have evolved to meet the available conditions, and there is no more significance to our lives than this. Dawkins' view is that the hypothesis of God is entirely superfluous and that order is due to natural selection alone — a blind, unconscious, automatic process' which is completely without purpose.[10] Hence the title of his book, *The Blind Watchmaker* in which he wrote:

> Evolution has no long term goal. There is no long distance target, no final perfection to serve as a criterion for selection ...The criteria for selection is always short term, either simply survival or, more generally, reproductive success ... The 'watchmaker' that is cumulative natural selection is blind to the future and has no long term goal.[11]

Richard Dawkins popularised the evolutionary and sociological principle of 'The Selfish Gene' (in his book by that name). According to this theory, people do things for the good of their

community or friends or even themselves, but their reasons for act-
ing in these ways is simply in order to enable human genes to sur-
vive. As Dawkins put it:

> We are survival machines — robot vehicles blindly programmed to
> preserve the selfish molecules known as genes.[12]

Some biologists such as Stephen Rose, Lichard Lewontin and Jay
Gould reject Dawkins view. They maintain that whole organisms and
species have a clear priority over our genes. However, Matt Ridley, in
The Origins of Virtue, considers that Dawkins' opponents have misunderstood the idea of the Selfish Gene, and he attempts to make the
position clearer. Ridley maintains that while human genes are undoubtedly selfish, humans have developed so that we have the ability
to over-ride our nature and to act virtuously in the interests of our
species as a whole. We are selfish in regard to the survival of our own
species — even against the best interests of other species and of the
planet itself — but within our species, altruism and even self-sacrifice
is in the genetic interests of our species.

Post-modernism would not be comfortable even with such clear
claims to 'the truth' about our genetic makeup and the origins of
the virtues as those made by Dawkins. With the Nietzschean version of post-modernism, we have come to the end of the road.
Philosophy, theology, art, music, literature and indeed science are all
folly. The most they can do is shock us out of complacency, force us
to break free from our conditioning, and see the world differently,
although not, of course, in any better way. There is no idea of
progress, of having advanced.

In a way, post-modernism is a logical outworking of Darwinian
evolution. Just as the theory of survival of the fittest holds that
'whatever is, is right', so the same applies in all other fields as well
as in biology. The confidence that was found in science in the sev-
enteenth and eighteenth centuries and among the Romantics of the
nineteenth century has vanished. As Dostoyevsky's Ivan Karamazov
says, with the death of God 'all is permitted'. There is no wrong and
no right; there is simply what we have in existence.

The French novelist, Albert Camus (1913–1960) tried to
understand how Ivan's rebellion against God in the name of
humanity could have ended in Stalin, Hitler and Pol Pot's death
camps. The answer is, of course, that if everything is indeed permitted, if morality has no grounds, if there are no values, then there

is no ground to condemn such atrocities except from within one's own culture. On this basis, those defendants at the Nuremberg trials who claimed that the trials were just the morality of the victors judging those of the vanquished were right. The prosecutors, of course, claimed that this was not the case. They were working with an Aristotelian form of morality grounded in a common human nature, which post-modernists would certainly reject. Richard Tarnas expressed it well:

> The situation recognised by John Dewey at the start of the century, that 'despair of any integrated outlook and attitude [is] the chief intellectual characteristic of the present age,' has been enshrined as the essence of the post-modern vision, as in Jean-Francois Lyotard's definition of post-modern as 'incredulity toward metanarratives'.[13] Here, paradoxically, we can recognise something of the old confidence of the modern mind in the superiority of its own perspective. Only whereas the modern mind's conviction of superiority derived from its awareness of possessing in an absolute sense more knowledge than its predecessors, the post-modern mind's sense of superiority derives from its special awareness of how little knowledge can be claimed by any mind, itself included.[14]

Post-modernism claims a position of superiority from which it rejects all the striving of philosophy to try to seek out ultimate truth. It can make seriousness about how life should be lived and about truth something to be derided — ideas whose time has passed and which are not worthy of serious discussion. This is, I want to argue, a radically mistaken attitude and it is one directly challenged by those neglected philosophers on which I shall draw in the third section.

12

POST-MODERNISM AND SELF-IDENTITY

Post-modernism can be seen as Cartesian doubt carried to its extreme — everything is doubted. There are, as we have seen, different views within post-modernism:

1. There are those, such as Rorty, who maintain that there is no such reality; there is only our radically contingent perspective.
2. On the other hand, there are those, such as Derrida, who maintain that there is a reality but language places an active role in forming our perspectives of reality, and there is no unmediated access to this reality. The way we make our world has consequences for the way we act within it. Derrida would reject the idea that one perspective can hold more truth than another. The most he would say is that some perspectives can be more significant than others, and what is significant is determined by the extent to which they show that they are merely perspectives. The more a perspective shows its own per-spectival nature, the more adequate it is.

In some senses post-modernism is the very opposite of the Cartesian enterprise which withdraws into a private, inner world of certainty. Our language mediates reality to us — there are echoes in Derrida's position of a Kantian noumenal world which is acces-sible only via frameworks of which we are a part. Text and reading thus becomes vital as it is necessary to remind ourselves that we have forgotten the language cages in which we are imprisoned and from which we cannot free ourselves. We can see other perspectives through reading but they are all partial. They are all stories rather than The Story and any move to construct a new story has to be resisted and undermined.

Post-modernism is about telling stories rather than The Story, refusing to allow the individual to be subsumed within a general, overarching story, refusing to write *the* history of the Second World War or *the* biography of Churchill. All we can write is stories that lead to more stories as truth is always perspectival and dependent on the interpretative structures through which it is viewed.

It would be a grave mistake to see post-modernism solely in negative terms. It has, particularly in its portrayal by Derrida and Levinas, many very important and positive insights which cannot be ignored. One of the most interesting issues is that the rise of post-modernism has been directly accompanied by and linked to the rise in the importance of gender and sexuality, the link that is not immediately obvious. These issues arise directly out of consideration of what it is to be an individual. They were made clearer to me by a paper given by Laurence Hemmings of Heythrop College, University of London, at a staff seminar in 1998.

THE QUESTION NOT THE ANSWER

One of the key issues in post-modernism is the identity of the person asking the questions. Post-modernists do not deny that 3 + 2 = 5 or that I am typing these words on a laptop, but they are interested in who the self or the 'I' is that is asking the questions to which answers are given. Descartes retreated into himself to arrive at certainty, and he grounded this certainty on what he regarded as metaphysical foundations. However, if it is accepted that 'God is dead' and with God are rejected all metaphysical foundations, then by reference to what does the 'self' construct or identify itself with or what constructs it? Post-modernism switches attention away from the disembodied 'I' to the identity of the embodied person who is asking questions — and embodiment inevitably lays stress on gender and sexuality as a crucial part of who we are. Individuals are different from each other because they have different bodies, different genders and different sexualities. Gender and sexuality are not necessarily the same. A woman may be sexually inclined towards other women, towards men or towards both men and women, and within these categories are many possible sub-divisions.

CONSTRUCTION OF TERMS

Central to post-modernism is the whole idea of difference. What differentiates us from each other is, in particular, our bodies, as well as many other factors, such as culture and language. Post-modernism can be seen as a celebration of difference and a resistance to the idea of any single view of what it is to be human.[1]

We are constructed by many factors outside our control including bodily factors. Descartes' idea of a self as a disembodied 'real I' has been rejected, with the position of the body and where it is placed being central. Post-modernism rejects the attempt to find a universal human nature and, in its absence, we have to find a new way of affirming our identity. It shows us that the terms to which we often appeal to affirm our identity are being displaced — their meanings are no longer fixed. As Laurence Hemmings pointed out, terms such as:

- woman
- family
- marriage
- country
- citizen

have no clear meaning any longer. A person may have a female gender and a male sexuality; 'family' may represent a single parent, two same-sex parents, a heterosexual parent or a complex interplay of diverse relationships. Marriage is less and less likely to be performed in church, and many people who are legally married may not consider themselves to be so, while those who are not may consider that they are. Understandings of what marriage represents varies widely between cultures and even within cultures. In some cultures marriage is an exclusive relationship between one man and one woman, while in others a man may marry four women. In some societies today men and women of the same gender may marry and the idea of 'common law' or 'de facto' marriage (in which a couple are treated as married even though no ceremony has been performed) has for centuries been accepted by law.

Even 'citizenship' and 'country' are terms which have been deconstructed and the idea of a single meaning is more and more undermined. What these terms mean is relevant to the culture and society in which we belong and the idea of any 'essence' of anything is precisely what is rejected.

Words like 'family' are slogans which are often used to impose a particular understanding on others. Talk of 'family values' does not appeal to a single view of what a family is. Rather, it seeks to impose a particular, narrow definition of a family, and by so doing seeks to marginalise other definitions. It is, therefore, an exercise in power.

Gender and sexuality have often more to do with power than anything else. Indeed, language and the idea of fixed meanings can be used by those in power to retain or spread this power. Sexual ethics has suddenly risen to prominence during the twentieth century with the rise in post-modernism because those in power (in church and state) wish to retain their power over those who do not conform to their stereotypes. It is important to recognise that according to post-modern view any one view of gender or sexuality is only a stereotype because the idea of any ultimate has been discarded. Males have traditionally defined what it was to be a female. Women were held to be incomplete and defective men, lacking the aptitude for spiritual matters which men possessed. Even today, some churches will not allow women to be priests. Once female identity and a variety of different sexualities are asserted, these are ways of subverting existing power structures and are accordingly considered to be threatening and dangerous.

Luce Irigaray is one influential modern writer who refuses to accept that woman should be identified by reference to man. Her approach can illuminate something of the post-modern position, although her approach, when analysed, is not a post-modern one.

LUCE IRIGARAY

Irigaray was born in France in 1930. She moved to Paris after the student riots of 1968 where she took up a post working for Lacan in psychoanalysis. She had close links with the Communist Party. The publication of her book *Speculum of the Other Woman* in 1974 led to her dismissal from her post with Lacan . The book was a feminist critique of the accepted psychoanalytic way of looking at human beings.

In 1986, Irigaray wrote a long review article on the recently released book by the feminist writer Elizabeth Schussler-Fiorenza. Irigaray praised the book but considered that it did not go far enough in its analysis or in the conclusions it reached. Schussler-Fiorenza claimed in her book that women were even more significant among the earliest followers of Jesus than the Gospels record, and that this influence and presence was deliberately played down and subverted in the interests of the male hierarchy which took up Jesus' message after his death. Schussler-Fiorenza claimed that it is the Greek/Roman world, with its strong patriarchal emphasis, that distorted the Jewish view of the importance of women in Jesus' ministry. She analysed the Christian texts and set out to show, by reference to allusions, omissions and implications, the many areas where the influence of women has been suppressed.

Irigaray was critical of Schussler-Fiorenza's enterprise on two main grounds:

1. It is not clear that, historically, women were as central as she claims. Jesus was, after all, a male and his disciples appear to have been male. Irigaray therefore maintained that, far from trying to read into the Gospel narratives a greater feminine presence than may be justified, a more radical conclusion is required, namely that Jesus can only be a partial revelation of God. If human beings are made in God's image and both male and female are in the image of God, then a human figure who is biologically male can only be a partial revelation of God.

2. Coming to subjectivity is an achievement; it is not something that happens automatically, and it is a process that necessarily involves culture. If, therefore, women live in a male dominated culture, the only way they can come to selfhood is effectively by becoming men, not by asserting their own selfhood as women.

Grace Jantzen, Manchester University, pointed out that Irigaray was heavily influenced by Simone de Beauvoir and she used Beauvoir as a basis on which to build her considerably more radical approach. De Beauvoir wrote: 'One is not born as a woman, one becomes woman.'[2] If a woman is to become a self, however, the only sort of self she can become in a masculine-dominated society is a masculine self since feminine selves do not exist. The point is that if the only form of identity in a society is a male identity, then women are either forced to emulate men or to completely lack an identity. De Beauvoir considered that the category of 'woman' is, in fact, a social construct of men and therefore to become a 'woman' is to enter into a category produced by males. She wanted women to transcend the categories of wife and mother (the reproductive categories) through which men have conceived them, and to achieve equality with men in the fields of art, literature, philosophy and politics.

It is here that both Schussler-Fiorenza and Irigaray differed from de Beauvoir because they saw women who do this as desexing themselves by entering into what is effectively a male version of selfhood. As an alternative, they called for women to work out what it is to be a woman independent of the categories males have created for them. We can see here the post-modern influence at work. By analysing the notion of identity of 'woman' it becomes clear that this identity is not autonomous but a social construct defined in male terms. Rather than accept this, women need to create a new identity for themselves which can define who they are as women and not in terms of their relation to men.

For de Beauvoir, men and women are equal and women must assert themselves to claim the position of equality which men have denied them for too long. In a way, de Beauvoir still maintained the idea of a single human nature to which both men and women equally aspire. This, however, failed to take into account the difference between men and women — not least the biological differences — and, if there is no such identity, is an approach that can easily be rejected. By contrast, for Schussler-Fiorenza and Irigaray, men and women are *not* equal; they are different. The sexual difference between men and women is not a mere incidental difference; it goes to the root of who they are.

St Augustine said that if God intended to create a companion for man, he would have created another man. Woman was needed primarily for reproduction. Indeed, As I argue elsewhere,[3] it was St Augustine's negative attitude to women that reinforced an already dominant view that subverted female identity and led to oppression. Religion, not only Christianity, has been a way of perpetuating this and denying women their sexuality.[4]

Crucial for Aristotle, for Aquinas who followed him and for the subsequent Natural Law tradition was the idea that all human beings shared a common human nature, a nature which Aquinas, not surprisingly, considered to be male. Men were the paradigm and, to the extent women did not fulfil this paradigm, they suffered a privation of the good that men had. Women were inferior both because they were 'defective males' and because women were passive in the sexual act. Aquinas, being a friar, may not actually have made love to a woman and may not have realised how very wrong he was. Aquinas did, however, consider that after death women and men will be treated equally, depending on their merits.[5]

One way to look at both Schussler-Fiorenza and Irigaray's positions is to see them as affirming the nature of women as women. There is not a single category or nature of human beings that both women and men can fulfil. Instead, the sexual difference between men and women goes to the very root of their nature. There are two distinct natures, and a woman cannot come to fulfilment of her nature by fulfilling the nature of a man.

Both Rene Descartes and John Locke, in their very different ways, held that being a self was something that was common to all humanity. 'I am a thinking thing' leaves little room for doubt that there is a subjective essence of an individual which constitutes his or her real identity. Freud showed, however, that a human being becomes a self through a socialisation process begun early in childhood. A self is, therefore, something that is created rather than something with which one is born. Grace Jantzen put this as follows:

> A human being begins life as a mass of conflicting desires: in order to become a unified subject, some of these will have to be repressed, thereby forming the unconscious, which may always threaten to erupt. Moreover, this unification, if it is to effect successful entry into society, will have to take place according to the norms of that society, which in the case of Western modernity are heavily masculine and heterosexual. Thus in Freud's account of the Oedipus stage the young boy under threat of castration represses his desire for his mother and tries to become like his father, eventually taking his father's place in society. The cost of this, however, is a denial of some of his most central longings, especially those for his mother. This denial may be so painful that it results in anger, fear or hatred towards anyone who reminds him of it; hence the misogyny and homophobia of Western modernity.[6]

Jantzen pointed out that, for both Freud and Lacan, being a woman is defined by a lack. Thus Freud said that a woman lacks a penis, and

Lacan said that a woman is 'not all'.[7] Both Freud and Lacan may well have been influenced, albeit perhaps sub-consciously, by the Aristotelian tradition. Irigaray rejected this and asked the more radical question as to how women can become subjective selves as women rather than fitting into the sociologically determined picture laid down by the male hierarchy. If the whole of society and the whole of our culture are determined by men, and if subjectivity comes into existence (and is not pre-existent) through conformity with society and the whole socialisation process, then women face an acute problem.

The inter-play between men and women, between feminists and those who oppose them, can be seen, according to this view, as a power-play between different forces. Each side is striving to create, affirm and achieve supremacy for their own models; and each is unwilling to submit to the models which 'the other', the different, seeks to impose. This is clearly a post-modern stance.

Women have to carve out selfhood for themselves by emphasising their difference and by refusing to conform to the male dominated models of the society in which they live. This, inevitably, will lead them to clash with the values of the society they inhabit, because to react against the norms of this society, particularly when these norms are generally accepted and are male, will provoke conflict. Women cannot even speak of what they are since their language — learnt in and representing a male culture — fails to give them a voice or even a language, which, too, have to be created. Irigaray seeks, therefore, to listen to the silence of women, to find the implicit voice of women beneath the explicit male language which they use. Again, Irigaray seems to imply that there is a woman's nature waiting to be discovered. It is not a single human nature that male and female share, nor is it a male nature that society maintains is androgynous. Rather, it is a latent, still to be discovered, lurking but nevertheless real nature. This in itself is significant as it seems to be clearly making a realist claim that there is a nature to be found. We have here a post-modern idea of relativity coupled with the claim that there is a truth at stake. We have a clear commitment to the view that there is an intrinsic nature which women can develop. This has lurked unnoticed and latent because of the dominance of men. Irigaray may or may not be right about the existence of this nature, but the fact that there is such a nature is closer to a position that Aristotle would have understood than to post-modernists. Irigaray, therefore, belongs to the strand of post-modernism of which Derrida and Levinas are also members — namely, one that is not nihilistic and relativistic, but quite the reverse.

An alternative view would be to hold that every person is unique and individual, made up of a complex network or relationships, cultural norms, sexual and gender paradigms, and so on. However, if this position is taken, then there is no such thing as 'woman'. The terms 'women' and 'men' only demarcate certain broad categories that pick out one of many differences. This may be closer to a true post-modern understanding but in this case each person has to work out for themselves how they have been constructed and then come to terms with this before trying to change it. This is an issue to which I shall return in the third section.

Irigaray does not dismiss theology, rather she seeks to reform it. Traditional theology has worked with a male God, represented by a male son, with male priests and a male language. This brings her to her second point that, given gender is constitutive of human nature and the male and female are distinct and have different natures, Jesus, as a male, cannot fully represent God. Jesus, necessarily, can only partly reveal God. The female side of God's nature is not revealed in Jesus. Clearly this has considerable theological implications, and the traditional idea of Jesus' place as the second person of the Trinity is radically undermined:

> Man has sought out a uniquely male God ... God has been created out of man's gender. He is Father, Son, Spirit. Man has not allowed himself to be defined by another gender: the female.[8]

> We have no female trinity. But as long as a woman lacks a divine made in her image she cannot establish her subjectivity or achieve a goal of her own. She lacks an ideal that would become her goal or path in becoming ... If she is to be a woman, if she is to establish her female subjectivity, a woman needs a god who is a figure for the perfection of her subjectivity.[9]

There has been an increasing trend to the painting of pictures of 'Christa' — the female figure on the cross of Andrew Boyd's 'Christa' and the Bosnian Christa are two of the best known recent examples although the Australian artist Josi Williamson also provides a striking example. If Jesus dies as a human being representing male and female, then a female figure on the cross represents this more clearly to a woman than a male figure. If Jesus is specifically male rather than human, then to paint Christ as a female would be offensive, but the more the maleness of Jesus is emphasised, the less effective the figure can be as a redeeming figure for half of humanity, namely women.

It is interesting that in the Roman Catholic Church there has been a movement to elevate the status of Mary in recent years. In 1953, it was proclaimed (as one of the very few dogmas) that all Catholics must hold that Mary was assumed into heaven directly. More recently, an increasing number of conservative Catholics are promulgating the idea that Mary is to be seen as an equal redemptrix of the world with Christ. Whatever the truth or falsity of these claims — and it is far from clear how such truth and falsity could be established other than by using anti-realist criteria — they do perhaps point to a perceived need to move towards a closer identification of a female figure with the deity, however limited the model of a woman who has never expressed her sexuality by intercourse, never had an orgasm, and never lost her virginity (in spite of the birth of a child) may be to women who want to find their own subjectivity.

Whether or not Irigaray's analysis is valid is not my concern. If she is right, however, then a total reappraisal of Christian liturgy, worship, theology and morality is called for so as to represent to women the female side of God. However, for my purpose the key point is that while Irigaray is a leading feminist and is often identified with post-modernism, the ontology of her position seems to be strictly realist. She is making claims about the truth of the human condition and the falsity of prevailing views of that condition. The scope for argument about the validity of her claims is immense, but my point is that the argument is about truth — about how human nature, or, if Irigaray is right, the different male and female natures, are to be seen and developed. As such, Irigaray seems to be in a direct line with Aristotle, Aquinas and the great realists of the past. She is not a relativist, and she is not an anti-realist — this is precisely what gives rise to her passion. Her books seek to show that she is right and that prevailing orthodoxy is wrong, and in this sense I agree with her that there is indeed a truth to be sought.

SUMMARY

It is possible to isolate some principles which underpin the post-modernist positions, although there is no single position that may be regarded as 'the' post-modern. The whole enterprise is vague, diffuse and complex and resists easy categorisation. However, broadly, the essential elements include the following:

1. Reality is a product of constant change and flux, of interpretation and reinterpretation. There are no fixed certainties, no objectivity.
2. Language plays an active role in forming our perceptions of reality and these perceptions govern who we are. There is no pure knowledge outside of society or culture or language and its symbolism.
3. Human beings are not separate from this reality, and there is no one reality. Instead, what we perceive and make sense of as real is itself ever changing.
4. Abstract principles, metaphysics and any search for a single truth or for any commitment to an ontology independent of our experience are to be rejected.
5. There are, and can be, no final truths, nor is there any possible idea of progress except in so far as we recognise progress, in so far as we recognise the perspectival nature of all we experience and communicate.
6. Gender differences are of vital importance in forming and interpreting reality. For too long, reality has been and still is constructed on male terms, and this has been and is used as a vehicle for oppression.
7. There needs to be greater emphasis on difference and a rejection of any idea of a single nature. Male, patriarchal, Western ideas and values deny difference and attempt to impose an artificial uniformity. There are clear links between this and Liberation Theology.
8. In art, science, aesthetics, literature, morality and religion, as well as in all other fields, there are no absolutes. At Harvard University, English students insisted that the Boston telephone directory should be placed on the reading list alongside the works of Shakespeare. To one version of post-modernism (not that of Derrida or Levinas), the one has no more intrinsic value than the other, just as a child's daub has no more value than a Picasso or a Constable, or the Spice Girls music has no more value than Mozart. Derrida and Levinas, by contrast, are motivated by a strong commitment to 'justice' and 'the other', and are quite the reverse of relativists.

Each of the above statements can be challenged and each can be shown to be possibly false or at least legitimately debatable. That, however, is not my task. My aim has been merely to outline one path leading away from Kant and to show how, through Hegel, Marx, Ivan Karamazov and Nietzsche, it has led to the sense of meaninglessness that many feel today. Instead of arguing against this, I want in the next section to outline an alternative path.

13

INTERIM CONCLUSION

We started with Kant and saw a tension present in his thought between wishing to give first place to reason and to sciencebut at the same time to leave space for God, and wanting to maintain that there is a real world, one that is completely unknowable. After Kant, two possibilities lay open:

1. to reject all ideas of a God who creates and sustains the universe, as well as all idea of a noumenal, real world; or
2. to affirm the idea of God and a real world.

After Kant, Hegel and Marx started the progress down one path by effectively rejecting God and making the real world lying behind the world we know irrelevant. Nietzsche took this further and rejected God entirely and with God any claim to truth at all. Nevertheless, he was not a total relativist and still saw truth in the claim that history led to the emergence of the Superman and to the understanding of the danger of Christianity and Christian morality. Dostoyevsky's Ivan Karamazov rebels against God in the name of humanity and, as he says, after rejecting God 'everything is permitted'.

Many modern philosophers tend to dismiss all ideas of a real world, with truth being radically perspectival. Some versions of post-modernism takes this trend further and we are left floating on a sea of meaninglessness, where truth is a dirty word or anyone's truth is as good as anyone else's.

In the first two sections of this book, a picture has been painted which leaves us intellectually vulnerable. God and metaphysics have been rendered irrelevant. Science is increasingly successful in explaining human beings in terms of the double helix that is their genetic pattern but leaving little or no room for meaning or value other than those meanings we create for ourselves. Anti-realism is persuasive in portraying religious truth claims as being true simply within the form of life that different religious believers inhabit.

This poses a real challenge for the way human beings see themselves. Although not directly aware of post-modern culture and deconstructionism, many young, and not so young, people implicitly share many of the assumptions of these movements and are affected by feelings of despair and futility that go to the heart of their lives. Yet few other alternatives present themselves.

Where do we go from here? What alternatives are there, if any? It is this challenge to which the third section will attempt a response.

The divide in the road after Kant can be sketched as follows:

KANT

Kant affirmed the distinction between the phenomenal and noumenal worlds. The phenomenal is the only knowable world while the noumenal is unknowable. God was needed as the guarantor of the fairness of the universe and to overcome evil within human beings.

HEGEL

Hegel still left a role for 'God' or Absolute Spirit which emerged in history and was dependent on human reason. He rejected Kant's noumenal world and substituted a study of history for theology.

MARX

Marx rejected God entirely and saw the triumph of working people as being inevitable through the onward march of history.

DENIAL of a REAL WORLD

The denial of Kant's noumenal, real world is taken further with the denial of any reality beyond that which humans construct. Language is a cage which constitutes the reality in which human beings live.

NIETZSCHE and IVAN KARAMAZOV

Nietzsche rejected God and Ivan rejected the world God made. 'Everything becomes permitted', and with the death of God also dies all meaning, value and purpose. Christian values such as love, compassion, pity and humility are denied in favour of the values of the strong.

POST-MODERNISM

Post-modernism is difficult to characterise but, broadly, there are two possible versions, both of which reject metanarratives. One view holds that human beings are afloat on a constantly changing sea where perspective is all. Culture, gender, sexuality, social station and other factors determine what is real, and truth is finally abandoned. According to the other view (Derrida, Levinas and others), texts and claims to truth must always be viewed with suspicion, but there is also strong a commitment to 'justice' and 'the other'. Post-modern culture leads to a denial of any absolutes and truth becoming a word of oppression. Every perspective is equally valid.

PART THREE

THE CENTRE
CAN HOLD

Turning and turning in a widening gyre
The falcon cannot hear the falconer;
Things fall apart; the centre cannot hold;
Mere anarchy is loosed upon the world.
The blood-dimmed tide is loosed, and everywhere
The ceremony of innocence is drowned.
The best lack all conviction, whilst the worst
Are full of a passionate intensity.

W.B.Yeats

The search for truth seems to be at an end. Post-modernism is the culmination of a movement that started with a divide in the road of intellectual history after Kant and now there seems to be no way forward. Anti-realism in religion and morality merely confirms the radical relativity of different truth perspectives and the younger generation, as well as those who are older, may come to despair at the lack of meaning and value in the world in which we live.

The third part of this book will go back in order to go forward, to recapture the alternative path that lay open after Kant. This is the path of Kierkegaard, Wittgenstein and Vaclav Havel. It is also the path of Rabbi Reb Menahem Mendl of Kotzk (the Kotzker) in Poland, possibly of the Sufi mystics and a minority of others. It is an unfashionable understanding of truth, a path that few espouse, but a path that still lies open and which can provide a way forward, provided the necessary conditions that it entails are accepted.

14

THE PATH TO TRUTH

This book seeks to chart a path between the rocks of fundamentalism and relativism. It seeks to maintain that the passionate intensity of the former should be rejected and that the centre can hold.

In the first part of this book the anti-realist challenge to a traditional, realist approach to religious, moral and other truth claims was set out. It was argued that the attempt to prove the existence of God fails and that an appeal to revelation, by use of Reformed Epistemology, also fails. The obvious alternative is anti-realism or, in psychology, constructivism, which allows each religious group to claim truth and only to appeal to their own stories and traditions to substantiate this truth. Truth is then based on coherence within a specific form of life.

The second part began with Kant and traced a path down one divide in the intellectual road through Hegel, Marx, Ivan Karamazov and Nietzsche, which leads to post-modernism and an even more radically relative understanding of truth. This renders the whole idea of a real world absurd and, with it, all talk of God.

The task in this third part is to consider how religious and moral realist truth claims can still be made in the face of the challenges presented by anti-realism and post-modernism. The history of religion has included claims to transcendence which go beyond a transcendence located solely within the human psyche or community. Yet such claims seem increasingly difficult, if not impossible, to justify. This part will maintain that traditional realist claims can still be made, but if they are made, they *necessarily* involve humility and ambiguity. If these qualities are absent, then the only conclusion is that those who lack these qualities are arrogant, bigoted, philosophically naive, intent on seeking power rather than truth or that they are anti-realists. These are harsh words but I will argue in this part that they can be demonstrated to be true. Many cults and new religious movements could be claimed to fit into one or other of these categories, as well as certain forms of evangelicalism in the Anglican Church, groups such as Opus Dei in the Roman Catholic Church, Hindu fundamentalists in India, certain right wing Orthodox Jewish groups in Israel and fundamentalists in Islam, whether they are the Taliban in Afghanistan, some Sunni Muslims in Iran or Shias in Iraq.

If a claim to truth in a realist sense is to be defended, then truth needs to be found in many quarters of the globe and not in one religious tradition alone. Any understanding of truth must not be confined to a particular revelation to a privileged group — truth is something that should, in principle, be accessible to all human beings. If this is denied, then a form of apartheid would exist with some human beings being confined, through no fault of their own, to ignorance or error, while a privileged group had access to truth. If there is any God, then this could scarcely be a just way of proceeding. I shall be drawing on Jewish, Christian and Islamic sources in this section but also on a contemporary politician, poet, philosopher and playwright.

The approach to truth advocated here has a long history, starting with Socrates and possibly even before him with the priests of the Greek god Apollo and the prophets of ancient Israel. 'Know Thyself' read the inscription over the Temple of Apollo at Delphi. Only as the individual turns away from obsession with the realm of the temporal can he or she begin to understand and approach truth. This was also Plato's position in his allegory of *The Cave*. Socrates, into whose mouth Plato put many of his own ideas, recognised in *Phaedrus* his inability to understand himself:

> I've not yet succeeded in obeying the Delphic injunction to 'know myself', and it seems to me absurd to consider problems about other beings while I am still in ignorance about myself.

For Socrates and Plato, truth was bound up with knowledge of oneself and philosophy was centrally connected with the personal search for truth. This search was costly and demanding; it involved seeing through the shadows of illusion present in the world around us. Socrates believed that one could seek knowledge both of truth and of oneself by the effort of one's own will.

The same position was held by Pelagius who opposed St Augustine and who, because he lost a crucial vote at an early Council of the Church, was condemned as a heretic. Augustine's view was that nothing was possible without the assistance of grace. In other words, divine aid was needed to overcome the effects of original sin. The human will was, therefore, permanently impaired and God's grace was needed to overcome the effects of sin. However, the priests of the god Apollo, Socrates, Pelagius and St Augustine all agreed that knowledge of the truth about oneself was a vital precursor to any understanding of truth.

A common view today is that truth does not matter but love, pity and compassion do. I want to argue against this view and instead argue for the reverse. Truth is the most fundamental thing of all. This was made clear in a dispute between two of the greatest influences on Hasidic Judaism, the Baal Shem Tov and the Kotzker.

THE KOTZKER

Truth is severe, hard, demanding.
Plato

The Baal Shem Tov[1] was a greater inspiration to Jews than anyone else in history except the great fathers of the Jewish faith. His view of what it was to be human was highly positive. Every human being was a dwelling place of God and God could be found in even the greatest sinner. The Baal Shem saw goodness everywhere and in everyone, and no-one and nothing was separated from God's loving activity. The Jewish Temple had been the traditional centre of Jerusalem, but the Baal Shem established a new centre, the rabbi. Human beings, he maintained, could really be the dwelling place of God. God did not need an earthly temple; he dwelt in the hearts and minds of human beings.

Although the Baal Shem founded the Hasidic movement, his status was greater than that of the movement itself. His reputation was so great that no-one challenged him, except for one man, Rabbi Reb Menahem Mendl of Kotzk,[2] known as the Kotzker. He opposed the Baal Shem by providing an alternative focus. The Kotzker stressed truth while the Baal Shem stressed love and compassion. Abraham Joshua Heschel (to whom I owe much of this chapter) in his book *A Passion for Truth* made clear the tension between the two:

> The Baal Shem Tov's intention was to prevent Jewish piety from hardening into mere routine. Yet his path also became a habit, a routine.

When first conceived, an idea is a break through, once adopted and repeated it becomes a cul de sac ... Faith had become a way of life immune to challenge and doubt.[3]

The Kotzker taught that truth:

... could be reached only by way of the utmost freedom. Such freedom meant not to give in to any outside pressures, not to conform, not to please oneself or anyone else ... He insisted that to get to the Truth man had to go against himself and society. The true worship of God ... was not in finding the Truth, but rather, in an honest search for it.[4]

The Kotzker, like the ancient prophets of Israel, preached angrily against the people. Whereas the Baal Shem inspired joy, love and hope, the Kotzker brought dread and contrition. For him, truth was the absolute and the highest, and lack of integrity and lies were the opposite of truth. Truth cannot be felt where lies and deceit are present. Most people do not care much for truth and human beings will do almost anything to prevent it emerging because truth is unsettling and uncomfortable, the very opposite of the secure life for which most people crave. Most people seek the comfort zone; they seek compromise and an accommodation with general opinion. The Kotzker contrasted this with the fearless commitment to truth:

Most religious thinkers have assumed that the predicament of man is due to his failure to obey the Law or to adhere to orthodox belief. Kierkegaard and the Kotzker saw its source in the ubiquitous pitfalls within the soul, in men's amazing disregard of their presence ... *Beware, they said, of too much faith, of blind belief in dogmas, of a willingness to weed out doubts rather than face them, for these speak an unhealthy self-assurance precluding a reaching out for God.* With incisive radicalism, the Kotzker set out to knock down the facades that thinkers have spent centuries constructing to protect man from the shattering recognition of the disparity between his desire for reward and contentment and religious demands for holiness and contrition ...[5]

The Kotzker insisted that each individual has to make up their own mind about whether or not God exists. If there is no God then human beings are the measure of all things, but if God exists, then it is God who is the final measure. In the latter case there can be only one Truth and one standard for right and wrong. As Heschel put it:

What begins in a lie ends in blasphemy ... Truth is often grey, and deceit is full of splendour. One must hunger fiercely after Truth to be able to cherish it ... Truth is severe, harsh, demanding. We would rather hide our face in the sand than be confronted by it.[6]

Many would claim that the attribute most closely identified with God is love, compassion or justice. The Kotzker maintained that it is *Truth*.[7] Truth is not something that human beings can arrive at; it is an insight[8] which must be striven for. As Heschel said:

> Mahatma Gandhi, one of the twentieth century's great seekers after justice, shared the insight of Kierkegaard and the Kotzker. On this point, he wrote, at the end of his autobiography, *'My uniform experience has convinced me that there is no other God than Truth'*.[9]

Albert Schweitzer had a similar insight when he said that one belief of his childhood he preserved with the certainty that he could never lose it was belief in truth. He was confident that the spirit generated by truth is stronger than the force of circumstances.

To claim that truth matters more than love and compassion is a major claim which needs examination. At a surface level it appears absurd. When human beings are suffering and in need, to stand to one side and to contemplate truth would be obscene. One can imagine a terrorist attack or a sudden illness striking a community. The first priority would clearly need to be to show compassion and care for those in need rather than to leave them unattended while investigating the truth behind the attack. However, such a simplistic analysis misses the essential point that the Kotzker was making.

To say that truth must be given priority is to refer not to any abstract idea of truth, still less to historical or scientific truth claims. The Truth whose supremacy is being claimed here is the truth about the human condition. This is also related to truth about the nature of the world — whether there is a God and a life after death, and, if both exist, what effect this has. For the Kotzker, as an Hasidic Jew, it was of course the truth of the Torah and what God required of human beings, but he was quite prepared to challenge the Torah in the service of Truth if this was necessary. To avoid or run away from the Truth about central issues of life and instead to be content with the comfort zone where oneself and other people are simply 'happy' is to deny something fundamental.

A parent's prime duty is not to make their children happy; it is to help them grow into adulthood. Sometimes this may mean the children are not happy. They may need to be given inoculations against future illnesses which may be painful, they need to be made to go to school and to do their homework even when they show no interest in doing so, they need to write 'thank you' letters when friends give them presents, and they need to be taught to be concerned for others and not simply for themselves. The journey to adulthood is often painful and a parent has to show a 'tough love' that looks for what is best for the child, and not for what the child may at the time think is best. This is one of the greatest challenges of being a parent as the child's understanding and that of the adult may well differ. Of course, it is to be hoped that childhood, school and every other aspect of a young person's life will be happy, but happiness is certainly not the highest value.

Western capitalist societies and the regimes of the former Soviet Union have this in common: they both tend to consider that the well-being of their citizens is directly related to their material well-being. Advertisers encourage this fiction by constantly emphasising the pleasures to be attained by buying products. Children are convinced that to aspire to the latest video games will bring happiness. At most, however, these may entertain for a short time. Boredom is a feature of our society and there is a perceived need to keep oneself occupied in order to hold boredom at bay.

To say that truth is to be prized more highly than compassion and love is to claim that the truth about the human condition must be faced however uncomfortable the cost may be. The Kotzker rejected all complacency. The religious complacency of so many Jews was anathema to him as was their security as the heirs of Abraham and the chosen people of God. This did not mean, of course, that he lacked compassion. The reverse was the case. However, he felt that to allow people to delude themselves was not caring for them but, in fact, patronising them by allowing them to accept an illusion. He lived a very simple life, stripping away everything that got in the way of a radical accountability to truth. He demanded that his followers should seek truth wherever it led and however uncomfortable the journey.

To live in the Truth may well demand a service to others which shows compassion and love (as it did for Albert Schweitzer), or it may be that this love may be shown in many other ways. Some people will show their dedication to truth by:

- caring for the basic needs of the most vulnerable
- trying to get children to challenge the preconceptions of their parents and their schools

- seeking to subvert the accepted wisdom of society by getting individuals to face uncomfortable realities
- helping others through counselling or psychological analysis to
  come to see the truth about their past and their present realty
- standing as a witness to truth against societies that ignore it or seek
  to oppress it.

To challenge one's own most cherished ideas of what is true is
uncomfortable and disorientating. Heschel told the story of a young
man who came to see the Kotzker because he was very concerned
about where his reading and his thoughts were taking him:

> Once a Hasid came to Reb Mendl with a problem. 'Rebbe I have
> terrible thoughts.'
>
> 'Well?' ...
>
> 'Sometimes I think there is neither judgment or judge, that the world
> is lawless, God forbid.'
>
> 'Why does it bother you so?' ...
>
> 'Rebbe, if the world has no purpose, of what use is the Torah? ... If the
> Torah is of no use, then all of life is meaningless. That troubles me
> enormously.'
>
> Reb Mendl replied: 'Since you are so deeply concerned, you must be
> an honest man, and an honest man is permitted to harbour such
> thoughts.'

Doubt about religious certainties will be part of a search for
truth, and it may be an uncomfortable part. It is always more comfortable to be a fundamentalist, and one of the reasons for the rise
of cults and some new religious movements as well as more extreme
forms of traditional religions is that many people yearn for certainty. When, therefore, someone comes along proclaiming that they
have 'the Truth' many will follow them. The Kotzker insisted that
such people had to be resisted.

The passionate commitment to truth and to the impact of truth
on every aspect of life is shared by the Kotzker and a number of
other figures to be explored in the remainder of this section. All
were *deep* thinkers for whom the problems of existence and life went
to the very heart of who they were. This is the very opposite of comfortable, 'cosy' religion. They were wholly committed to seeking
truth and living truth but none ever claimed to have found it.
Heschel explained the position well:

'Mundus vult decipi' — The world wants to be deceived. To live without deception presupposes standards beyond the reach of most people whose existence is largely shaped by compromise, evasion and mutual accommodation. Could they face their weakness, their vanity and selfishness, without a mask? Could they bear the discovery that they had lived for goods they had never believed in or cherished, that they had been committed to ideas they had never been convinced of? The Kotzker realised these difficulties, that was why he was concerned only with the few. He surely recalled the outcry of Rabbi Shimon ben Yohai, the master in whose path he had decided to lead his own disciples: 'I have seen men of greatness, and they are but few.' Flowers turn to the light and grow. Owls avoid it and sleep. We are part flower, part owl. When light comes to us as a challenge and a demand, the owl in us is shocked and we turn away. When the urge to grow prevails, we welcome the challenge and the demand. The Kotzker sought to live by the unconditional challenge and dared to utter it. But this privilege was bought at a price: estrangement from his community.[10]

Seekers of truth — those who seek to live in the Truth — may often be outsiders to their communities, uncomfortable gadflies who challenge the status quo. Socrates was a gadfly as was the Kotzker and Soren Kierkegaard.

SOREN KIERKEGAARD AND SUBJECTIVITY

KANT AND THE SUBSEQUENT DIVIDE

Kant's rational approach has had a tremendous effect on subsequent philosophy and theology and, following him, there have been two major branches. As has been shown, Kant held to:

1. a distinction between the real, noumenal world which is unknowable and the world as we experience it which can be known but may not be real;
2. the claim that human beings are free and autonomous and can use the freedom of their wills to 'create themselves' and to develop a good will. However, once evil maxims had been adopted and become the ground of a person's will, then he or she could not release themselves of their own choosing and divine intervention is required.

One path branching from Kant, as we have seen, has:

1. rejected not only the idea of an unknowable real world behind the world of our experience, but, even more significantly, sometimes maintained that there is no real world at all, only the world as we construct it. If this position is adopted, then the very idea of truth becomes a fiction.
2. rejected the whole idea of God and, with it, any metaphysical ground for reality. This leaves human beings entirely alone and

completely autonomous, able to decide who and what they will become largely by arbitrary choice.

These conclusions follow only if one strand leading from Kant is taken. However, there is another, represented in the work of Soren Kierkegaard and continued with Ludwig Wittgenstein.

DESPAIR

Soren Aabye Kierkegaard lived in a Denmark dominated in intellectual circles by the philosophy of Hegel. Kierkegaard rejected Hegel's whole approach, root and branch. He considered it to be nonsensical, naive and foolish in the extreme. He was a philosophic realist in the classic tradition. Whereas Hegel is sometimes referred to as 'Both/And' because of the importance he attached to the dialectical process (see p 76), Kierkegaard is 'Either/Or'.[1] *Either* God exists *or* God does not. *Either* Jesus was God Incarnate *or* he was not. Kierkegaard allows no ambiguity. There is a truth at stake which cannot be compromised.

Whereas the strand from Kant which led through Nietzsche and onto post-modernism rejected a real, noumenal world and rejected God, Kierkegaard affirmed both. Kierkegaard was a thorough realist. He affirmed bivalence which, as we saw in the first part of this book, is the realist position which claims that statements are either true or false depending on the state of affairs to which they refer. In particular, he affirmed that there are historical and other truths which, while they may never be known with certainty, are nevertheless either true or false. In taking this position he challenged the whole post-modern, anti-realist, perspectival approach to truth. He was quite prepared to accept that there may be no God, but he insisted that there is a truth to be affirmed, or rejected.

For Kierkegaard, the temporal realm cannot provide hope; it can only lead to despair. This was a major claim and one that many will reject. His claim was that whatever the goal sought, whatever the life lived, underneath almost all lives lurks a despair that may be unnoticed, ignored, suppressed or denied but which is nevertheless real. Despair is closely connected with the idea of being or becoming a self. Many people are not selves at all. Instead of living their lives, their lives live them, and all they want to do is to conform, to be like others, to be accepted and not to be noticed. This leads to:

another kind of despair [which] allows itself to be, so to speak, cheat-
ed of its self by 'the others'. By seeing the multitude of people around
it, by being busied with all sorts of worldly affairs, by being wise in the
ways of the world, such a person forgets himself, in a divine sense forgets his own name, dares not believe in himself, finds being himself
too risky, finds it much easier and safer to be like others, to become
a copy, a number, alone with the crowd. Now this form of despair
goes practically unnoticed in the world. Precisely by losing himself in
this way, such a person gains all that is required for a flawless perfor-
mance in everyday life, yes, for making a great success out of life.
Here, there is no dragging of the feet, no difficulty with his self and its
infinitising, he is ground as smooth as a pebble, as exchangeable as a
coin of the realm. Far from anyone thinking him to be in despair, he
is just what a human being ought to be. Naturally the world has no
understanding of what is truly horrifying ...[2]

It is 'truly horrifying' that an individual has lost themselves in
conforming to their peers. They have lost any sense of self. It was
this that Tolstoy portrayed in his story *The Death of Ivan Illyich*. A
young man qualifies as a lawyer, progresses to being a magistrate,
then a judge. He marries and lives in a house like any other, fur-
nishes it like other houses, plays bridge and golf with his friends and
in every way conforms. It is only in the last three months of his life
as he is dying that he realises that he has lost his self completely, and
it is only at this time that he begins to recover it. As Kierkegaard
said:

In his ignorance of his own despair a person is furthest from being
conscious of himself as spirit. But precisely this — not being conscious of oneself as spirit — is despair, that is to say spiritlessness ...
the despairer is in the same situation as the consumptive; he feels
best, considers himself to be healthiest, can appear to others to be in
the pink of condition, just when the illness is at its most critical.[3]

Rudyard Kipling, in a poem called 'Tomlinson' depicts the fate
of someone who never becomes a self at all. Tomlinson dies and
goes to Heaven but is turned away at the gates because he has never
done anything that others have not done; he has lived secondhand.
He has never been in any sense a self and had not done anything
worthy of admission. However when he comes to Hell, the Devil
does not want him either because he has never been enough of a self
to sin; he has simply conformed. The Devil finally drives him back
to his body in the hope that he may become something worthy of
surviving death.

To take oneself seriously and to try to work out what truth means for each individual is essential. One cannot do that, however, by merely conforming to one's society, peer group, parents or teachers. Each person first has to wake up to the need to take themself seriously. This is not easy, nor is it something that most people want to do. Most people seek to lose themselves in activity and busyness, and forfeit the search for truth. As Kierkegaard said:

> In general, the urge for solitude is a sign that there is after all a spirit in a person and the measure of what spirit there is. So little do chattering nonentities and socialisers feel the need for solitude that, like love-birds, if left alone for an instant they promptly die. As the little child must be lulled to sleep, so these need the soothing hushaby of social life to be able to eat, drink, sleep, pray, fall in love, etc. It isn't only in the middle ages that people have been aware of this need for solitude, but also in antiquity there was respect for what it means; while in the never-ending sociality of our own day one shrinks from solitude to the point of not knowing to what use to put it to except (oh! excellent epigram) the punishment of law breakers. Yet it is true, in our own day it is indeed a crime to have spirit.[4]

In our impatient age, the idea of being silent and still and, even more, the idea that this can be a truth to be found in silence is alien to us. Children live in a world where they are surrounded by noise and activity and where they never have a chance to be quiet. In adulthood, activity dominates our lives. Despite being surrounded by supposedly 'labour-saving' devices there is a tendency to work long hours and to be involved in more activity than ever in the past except, perhaps, for collapsing in front of the television. Far from this yielding a greater understanding of truth and wisdom, the result is likely to be exactly the opposite. Yet if this happens, all the activity and busyness may be simply wasted in triviality:

> So much is spoken about wasting one's life. But the only wasted life is the life of one who has so lived it, deceived by life's pleasures or its sorrows, that he never became decisively, eternally, conscious of himself as spirit, as self ... so many live their lives in this way ... when the hour glass has run out, the hour glass of temporality, when the worldly tumult is silenced and the restless or unavailing urgency comes to an end, when all about you is still as it is in eternity — whether you are man or woman, rich or poor, dependent or free, happy or unhappy; whether you bore in your elevation the splendour of the crown or in humble obscurity only the toil and heat of the day ... eternity asks you and every one of these millions of millions, just one thing;

whether you have lived in despair or not ... if you have lived in despair, then whatever else you win or lose, for you everything is lost, eternity does not acknowledge you, it never knew you, or, still more dreadful, it knows you as you are known, it manacles you to your self in despair.[5]

A 17-year-old schoolgirl, Leanne Symes, in Dorset in England wrote the following parable in one of her lessons on 16 January 1999, which expresses a similar point:

The parable of the Tunnel

It began like this; a man began to walk, getting faster and faster and ignoring more and more of what was going on around him. Eventually he found himself in a tunnel. The tunnel was long and dark, there was not even a glimmer of light at the end. The man continued to walk.

Had he stopped to discover, he would have found that the walls of the tunnel were transparent, so if he had stopped he would have seen the bright, light-filled world of variety around him. Still he continued to walk, getting faster and faster.

Had he stopped to listen, he would have been told the way out and yet he continued to walked further and faster into darkness.

Perhaps then we should remember that when we find ourselves in a tunnel long and black, we should stop, look, listen and discover freedom from the narrowness of life in the tunnel.

Kierkegaard considered that a human being could only avoid despair by living their lives in truth, and to do this meant living life in relation to God. Only living in this way could provide the path to truth. Unlike Nietzsche who thought that God was dead, Kierkegaard reacted to the tension left by Kant about the place of God by making God central. Nietzsche thought that the death of God marked the death of all value and meaning. In affirming the centrality of God, Kierkegaard also maintained the fundamental importance of some ultimate value and meaning. He considered that one can only come to full humanity by living in right relation to God.

TRUTH AS SUBJECTIVITY

Kierkegaard, unlike almost any other theologian, refused to study theology that involved talking about God. He considered Systematic Theology of the type taught in theology faculties around the world to be folly. God, for Kierkegaard, was 'the Unknown' and he refused to speculate about the nature of God. This is very similar to the position taken by St Thomas Aquinas, although Aquinas, unlike Kierkegaard, thought that God's existence could be proved. Kierkegaard thought such an attempt was absurd. Aquinas also thought that language could be used about God.[6] Both Kierkegaard and Aquinas were ontological realists and both believed that truth claims of religion referred to the Unknown, on which the universe depends and which many name as God.

Kierkegaard thought that faith represented an unproved and unprovable assumption that the Unknown (which he termed 'God') existed and that living in truth means living in relationship to this reality. He rejected the attempt to arrive at truth objectively, as any such attempt will only be an approximation and will never be certain enough to serve as a basis for one's life. Faith precisely involves subjectivity as it means an inner appropriation of a commitment to a relationship. In a way it is like love — being able to talk about one's beloved is not the same as loving him or her. Concentration on the objective facts about God or ultimate reality yields nothing except objective facts, and certainly does not yield the transformation of a human life.

Religious faith does not stand on truth claims about the nature of God. The epistle of James says: 'You believe in God? You do well. The Devils also believe and tremble.' In other words, the devils believe that God exists, but they do not 'believe in' or centre their lives on God. Similarly, ultimate commitment to moral values does not depend on working out some ethical theory. Many moral philosophers develop and write or lecture about ethical theories but this does mean that they stake their lives on these theories.

Kierkegaard wished to move people away from the usual, objective way of talking about truth. Those who read this book may well have been expecting a discussion on the nature of objective truth, but for Kierkegaard such a discussion was uninteresting. Propositions may express something of the reality of the universe, whether in terms of history, science or other areas, but they cannot capture fundamental truths on which an individual might stake his or her life.

Kierkegaard's complaint was against philosophers, theologians and others who busy themselves building up more and more learning and lose touch with the simple. In particular they lose touch with the essential nature of truth and fail to address the really important issues such as what it means to live. A person can become so stuffed with theological or philosophical knowledge that he or she never gets round to *living* the simple life of faith. Human beings busy themselves with worldly, temporal tasks and so lose interest in questions such as 'How should I live?' or 'What does it mean for me to have faith?'. These can mistakenly seem, with much learning, to become irrelevant.[7] Such vital questions concern both young and old alike and have traditionally been at the very heart of philosophical reflection, yet, today, they are considered somewhat naive and unworthy of debate by academic theologians and philosophers. Indeed, today's philosophers rarely comment on any of the central issues of our day, which is a reflection of the way in which the discipline has largely become irrelevant to the lives of most people. This point was made by Pope John Paul II in his encyclical 'Fides et Ratio'. Kierkegaard argued that most philosophers are good academic talkers and writers yet fail to express anything significant with their lives. As he said:

> The police thoroughly frisk suspicious persons. If the mobs of speakers, teachers, professors, etc., were to be thoroughly frisked in the same way, it would no doubt become a complicated criminal affair. To give them a thorough frisking — yes, to strip them of the clothing, the changes of clothing ... to frisk them by ordering them to be silent, saying: Shut up, and let us see what your life expresses, for once let this be the speaker who says what you are.[8]

Instead of living in a world of words that have ceased to have any impact, philosophers, theologians and teachers should be judged by how they live. *An individual's life is the best expression of what he or she believes* — not the words that are said. Indeed, Kierkegaard wished people to be silent, to cease to take refuge in language and instead to consider who they are before God.

'Truth is subjectivity' is an ambiguous phrase. It is often taken to mean that whatever someone believes in passionately becomes true for them. This was Sartre's understanding and led to the importance he attached to personal authenticity. It is a reasonable but superficial reading of 'truth as subjectivity'. After all the very word 'subjectivity' seems to imply personal opinion and is a denial of the objective certainty on which any claim to 'objective' truth rests. If truth is, indeed, subjectivity then it seems that all Kierkegaard is calling people to is to live out whatever they see to be the Truth. If this is the case the very idea of truth collapses into personal opinion. However, this is not Kierkegaard's meaning. He maintains the realist position that:

1. *either* there is the Unknown, termed God, which is the ultimate source of value, and on which the universe depends
2. *or* there is not.

And in the case of Christianity:

1. *either* Jesus was God in human form
2. *or* he was not and was a normal, if remarkable, man such as Socrates.[9]

None of the above statements can be proved. None of them can be *known* to be true, but this does not to say that they may not be true. Kierkegaard was an ontological realist but epistemologically he accepted that we have no guaranteed access to the Truth. This does not mean, however, that we can be indifferent to it. Rather, we have to stake our life on a claim to truth even though this may not be provable.

This is a departure from Kant who was epistemologically an idealist and thought we could make truth claims only about the world of phenomena. Kierkegaard disagreed. We can make transcendent truth claims but they are not provable. Instead, we have to stake our lives on these claims with a passion and commitment that staking one's life necessarily involves, but also with the knowledge that they could be wrong. He quoted Socrates against those who thought it possible to prove the idea of a life after death. Kierkegaard thought this absurd, but he considered that Socrates presented the position well. Socrates said: 'I cannot prove the immortality of the soul, but I am ready to stake my life on this "if".' Similarly, a religious believer cannot prove that God exists but is willing to stake his or her life on this claim. Thus a Christian might say: 'I cannot prove that God exists or that Jesus was God in human form but I am ready to stake my life on this "if".'

CORAM DEO

Kierkegaard was a Lutheran, and one of Luther's key beliefs was the idea of the individual living life 'Coram Deo', 'in the heart of God' or directly before God. Luther considered that no human being was able to be virtuous by their own efforts. However hard one tries, one will fail to live up to the ideal. It is therefore necessary for the person of faith to trust totally in the love of God and the grace of God. All human beings are, in Luther's eyes, sinners — they are failures. However, if one tries to live one's life 'Coram Deo', then this cannot be done in part — one cannot come before God for an hour on Sunday. The whole of life has to be lived in the presence of God and as if God was an onlooker of one's everyday actions. No-one, Luther maintained, can expect that their actions will earn God's love. This love is an unconditional gift and the problem the individual faces is to be able to accept this love and then to try to live as if they are worthy of it. It is not possible to do more than this, and religious faith requires nothing less than to stake one's whole life on the claim that God exists and that one is accountable to God.

Karl Rahner, one of the most influential Jesuit theologians of the twentieth century, made a similar claim and affirmed the centrality of truth:

> In certain circumstances a person may ... be able to arrive at and affirm a truth, precisely as truth, in the depths of his actual accomplishments of life, even when he thinks himself obliged to deny it in his consciously formulated concepts, or knows nothing of it explicitly.

As Karen Kilby put it:

> Rahner's view is now what he describes as the usual modern one, namely that if a person is well-meaning and acting in good conscience, *it does not matter* whether they have latched onto the truth or not. Instead he maintains that if a person is well meaning and acting in good conscience they have in fact latched on to the truth, whether they have appeared to do so or not.

This is remarkably similar to Kierkegaard's view that truth is subjectivity and emphasises the importance of individual responsibility and a willingness to live in the truth.

Wittgenstein, in a very different way, reached a similar conclusion to Kierkegaard.

WITTGENSTEIN AND PERSPICUITY

THE SEARCH FOR PERSPICUITY

The idea of a perspicuous understanding is central to Wittgenstein's early and late work.[1] The Australian philosopher, Felicity McCutcheon, argued that this is a clear indication that his purpose in doing philosophy remained the same throughout his life. She wrote:

> However one characterises the changes within Wittgenstein's thinking, the concept of perspicuity and the need for clarification are continuous themes. They are central to Wittgenstein's first treatise (Wittgenstein 1922:4.003 and 6.54) and clearly evident in his last (Wittgenstein 1958:122,133). Not only are they continuous themes, but their content or target remains unchanged, suggesting that the point of Wittgenstein's remarks was also unchanging; that his purpose in doing philosophy was essentially the same throughout his life. Our central aim in this section is to develop a deeper sense of what that purpose was and show how it was, for Wittgenstein, connected to the concept (and pursuit) of perspicuity.[2]

Wittgenstein wished his own books could have been dedicated to the greater glory of God. He did not dedicate them in this way, not because of any personal scruples but because he felt that he would have been misunderstood. Wittgenstein bemoaned the scientific age in which he (and we) live, not because he disapproved of science, but, on the contrary, because the scientific outlook on the world is an impoverished one if it is the only way of looking at the world. In fact, he went as far as to say that poetry was his preferred method of doing philosophy, perhaps because poetry is so clearly of a different genre from science. Although the purposes underpinning his philosophy may not have changed between his earlier and later works, his focus did seem to shift. He was an original mind and his works are free from the quotations from other writers common in most books of philosophy. In his early works he quoted Frege and Bertrand Russell, but in his later works he quoted only from St Augustine and William James' book *Varieties of Religious Experience.*

Wittgenstein wished to dissolve problems that confronted philosophers. He thought the most thorny problems with which philosophers were confronted were, in fact, pseudo-problems and perspicuity was needed to see this. Once these problems could be seen correctly, they disappeared. It was not that they were resolved by a new theory, rather the problems were seen not to be problems at all.

In the first part of this book, Wittgenstein's treatment of Moore's propositions was discussed. It was seen that Wittgenstein showed that human beings are educated into a form of life for which there are no foundations other than what is done by those who participate in it. Once this is recognised, the search for foundations is seen as folly and the philosophic enterprise on which this search is based comes to an end.

McCutcheon quoted a paper by James Conant[3] in which Conant showed how similar the approaches of Wittgenstein and Kierkegaard's pseudonymous writer, Johannes Climacus, are. For both authors their aim was not to come to some conclusion which could neatly be summarised by commentators. Instead, it was to help their readers come to realise, to see something which they had not previously seen. This is Kierkegaard's whole art of indirect communication, to try to bring people to a new level of understanding, which is incredibly difficult to achieve. Kierkegaard, writing of his own work, said:

> An illusion can never be destroyed directly, and only by indirect means can it gradually be removed ... a direct attack only strengthens a person in his illusion. There is nothing that requires such gentle handling as an illusion, if one wishes to dispel it ... That is what is achieved by the indirect method which ... arranges everything dialectically for the prospective captive, and then shyly withdraws.[4]

In a way I am disregarding this advice (although I agree with it) as part of the aim of this book is to help religious people who are confident of their certainties to come to recognise that it is precisely these certainties which may be an illusion. Wittgenstein wishes to bring his readers to a perspicuous understanding, an idea that has links with the more traditional idea of wisdom.

The word 'wisdom' occurs 247 times in the Hebrew scriptures, and there are 47 references in the New Testament. Although in Genesis 3:6 Eve is portrayed as being tempted by the fruit that would bring wisdom and in some of Paul's epistles human wisdom is portrayed as empty in comparison to God's wisdom, in almost every other case there is praise for the search for wisdom. Solomon asked God for wisdom and because he asked for this gift God gave him all those things for which he did not ask. Job links age with wisdom and understanding and sees wisdom as being a defining characteristic of God.[5] In fact, he rejects his so-called comforters with their solid theology and tells them that if they were silent this would be closer to wisdom. The Psalms, the Wisdom literature, the book of Ecclesiastes and many more repeatedly speak of the search for wisdom. In the New Testament, people were amazed at the wisdom of Jesus.[6] As a young child, Jesus is noted and is praised for his wisdom.[7] God is described as wisdom itself and the source of all wisdom.[8] Wisdom needs to be prayed for and is given by God.[9]

The Greek word for wisdom is 'sophia' and it is, perhaps, significant that it is regarded by many feminist writers today as a feminine rather than a masculine attribute. The search for truth and moral rules in isolation can be regarded as a somewhat arid masculine enterprise which tries to tie down both religion and morality into firm categories. Wisdom and relationships, by contrast, require a more holistic approach. The story is told of a man who could take a flower and pluck every part of it naming every one, but what he could not see was the beauty of the flower because he lacked the wisdom to see the unity. Some scientists today think that human beings can be defined solely in terms of their genome and that, once the whole of the human genome has been mapped, we will be able to understand what it is to be human. They are like the man and the flower. Sometimes philosophers can behave the same way when considering the issue of truth. They can dissect language and life into such narrow categories that they lose sight of wisdom. 'Sophia' requires a broader perspective than the narrow, analytic approach to philosophy which has for too long dominated Western thought.

Wittgenstein was not trying to put forward a philosophic doctrine. This is the mistake that many commentators make when reading his work. They are looking for a new theory and Wittgenstein was precisely trying to resist theories. He wished people to stop doing philosophy rather than to produce a new philosophic theory. To do this, he tried to get them to 'see' something, to be perspicuous, to have insight, to be wise, to exercise 'sophia'. If they did, then what formally seemed to be philosophic problems amenable to analysis by theories would be seen in a different category entirely. This does not mean, however, giving up the search for truth, nor does it mean stopping being immensely *serious* about life and how it should be lived. Quite the reverse.

Wittgenstein wished to stop people doing metaphysics, but he had great respects for those serious philosophers of the past who grappled with the problems of life and arrived at metaphysical solutions. He admired their efforts and the integrity of their attempts, but contrasted them with the shallowness of professional philosophers today. He did not think that metaphysics was any longer relevant because the very enterprise of attempting to reason metaphysically is based on an illusion, a mistaken apprehension of the purpose and aim of philosophy. However, he wanted to reintroduce a seriousness into the study of philosophy and a new realisation of its profound importance.

We naturally tend to adopt a particular way of looking at the world, but Wittgenstein wanted us to see the danger of equating the 'natural' way in which we see the world with 'the truthful' way of seeing the world. He wished to do so by showing alternatives. As McCutcheon put it:

> Our tendency to accept general explanations, the 'naturalness' with which we do so is something we need to become aware of according to Wittgenstein, because it can lead to injustices. We are particularly attracted to explanations of the form: 'This is really only this'. Wittgenstein cites the easy acceptance of Darwin's theory as an example:
>
> 'One circle of admirers who said: "Of course" and another who said "Of course not" ... Why in the hell should anyone say "Of course"? ... Did anyone see this process happening? No. Has anyone seen it happening now? No. The evidence of breeding is just a drop in the bucket.

> But there were thousands of books in which this was said to be the obvious solution. People were certain on grounds which were extremely thin.' (Wittgenstein 1966:26)
>
> It is important to note that Wittgenstein is not commenting on whether the theory of evolution is actually true or false (although he may have objected to the way in which followers of Darwin transformed the theory from a principle of scientific explanation into a metaphysics of nature). He is interested in our tendency to see things in certain ways and the consequence this has for philosophical thinking in particular. As we shall see, the purpose of his own work was to undermine the tendency to say 'it must be like this' by providing alternatives which we had not thought about. His method is to change the way we think by helping us understand the way we adopt theories.

Wittgenstein helps people to see that when they so firmly assert truth, they may only be seeing a partial and incomplete picture which comes from a distinctive perspective. This is not to say, however, that there is no truth to be sought.

A search for wisdom involves, as the Kotzker, Kierkegaard and Wittgenstein clearly recognised, a change in oneself. Only the wise person can be wise, while a foolish person may know something true — even though this may be trite. Kierkegaard told the story of a man who escaped from an asylum and wanted to prove to everyone that he was sane so he went around saying 'Bang, the earth is round'. Undoubtedly this was true, but by reciting it he showed how deranged he was. So it may be with many today who concentrate on truth at the expense of wisdom. The wise person is not the same as the clever or the intelligent person, nor the person who knows many 'truths'. This is why Wittgenstein and Kierkegaard had so much contempt for professional philosophers. Both men saw little wisdom there, little real sense of a constant struggle to understand.

A philosopher should be someone who knows nothing and is troubled to the depths of their being by their ignorance. Too few modern, professional philosophers are disturbed and troubled in this way. Wittgenstein had a great admiration for those metaphysicians of the past who struggled to find a way of understanding knowledge and reality. These individuals showed passion and commitment to the search which they pursued with integrity and with every fibre of their being. By contrast, many modern philosophers are merely clever.

WAS WITTGENSTEIN AN ANTI-REALIST?

There are those who misinterpret Wittgenstein's ideas and it is very easy to see him as an advocate of anti-realism. Indeed, those who may be held to be in the anti-realist camp, such as Don Cupitt, Dewi Phillips and Gareth Moore,[10] constantly quote Wittgenstein (and Kierkegaard!). Wittgenstein rejected metaphysics when it is used to try to prove the foundation of our knowledge claims. He did not consider that Natural Theology succeeded. Wittgenstein showed that the form of life in which we live is expressed in language, and that we learn the grammatical rules that govern our understanding of morality and religion at an early age:

> ... when a child is first taken to Church, he has no religious experiences. They come later. What happens is that he is introduced to a context of ritual and worship ...[11]

We are educated into a form of life and it is by means of this that we make sense of our world. It provides a framework of understanding:

> Church doctrines are communally authoritative teachings regarding beliefs and practices that are considered essential to the identity of welfare of the group in question. They may be formally stated or informally operative, but in any case they indicate what constitutes faithful adherence to a community.[12]

It is true that, in this sense, theology can be seen as being based on the rules of grammar, the way in which language is used. Phillips gives expression to this view, as can be seen in a few quotations where Phillips is criticising the Systematic theologian, George Lindbeck:

> Lindbeck's own suggestion is that theological doctrines should be compared to grammatical rules. He echoes Wittgenstein's remark that theology is a kind of grammar. Theological doctrines become regulative rules for the use of the word 'God', not descriptions of an object given independently of themselves.[13]

> ... Lindbeck wrongly concludes that seeing theology as a kind of grammar entails not talking of God as an independent reality and ceasing to make truth claims concerning him. All that follows from the analysis, in fact, is that such talk should be understood within the grammar of the religious discourse in which it is made. All we are rescued from is the confusion of thinking that the notions of 'independent reality' and 'truth' in this context have the same grammar as they do in others.[14]

There are times when Lindbeck seems to appreciate this momentous fact. It is momentous because in saying 'God is love' one is providing a rule for the use of the word 'God' ... At other times, however, Lindbeck reverts to the tempting charm of the cognitive theory and speaks as though a truth concerning God has to do with the relation between the grammatical rule and a reality independent of itself. But this is to misunderstand the sense of the very notion of grammar Lindbeck wants to employ in referring to doctrines. Here is a good example of Lindbeck oscillating between, and thereby confusing, the two different grammars:

'... if the form of life and understanding of the world shaped by an authentic use of the Christian stories does in fact correspond to God's being and will, then the proper use of CHRISTUS EST DOMINUS is not only intersystematically but ontologically true. Utterances within any not totally incoherent religion can on this account be intersystematically true, but this in no sense assumes their ontological truth or meaningfulness.'[15]

Lindbeck is speaking as though he had introduced us to a conception of truth (which he calls ontological truth) which has an application independently of religion and independent of any form of life we could specify. Of course, it is no accident that he can give no substance to this conception ... Lindbeck states, quite clearly, the grammatical status of religious doctrines, and how these doctrines set the parameters for the discourse and identity of a religious community.[16]

This dispute between Phillips and Lindbeck goes to the heart of the issue of truth in religious and moral discourse. Phillips claim is that talk of an 'ontological truth' independent of language is meaningless. Theology is concerned with the grammar of language about God and the truth of theological language depends on the system within which these statements are made. The only reality to which this language refers is the reality found within the language itself. To the believer, 'God exists' is indeed true and what makes it true is that it has meaning and use within the community of belief. This does not mean, for Phillips, that there is any substance or being called God to which the language refers. If there was no language, if there were no believers, there would be no substance or reality called God. Phillips thinks he is being faithful to Wittgenstein when he says this, but he is not.

Wittgenstein makes a distinction between *empirical* and *grammatical* statements. Empirical statements are those that can be verified and are akin to scientific statements. Phillips rejects all attempts to establish the existence of God by reason or to ground religious beliefs as if they were empirical claims:

> ... in countless philosophy classes, the traditional arguments associated with theism are subjected to devastating criticisms. The traditional proofs for the existence of God which, arguably, began as attempts to understand the Faith from within it, are now made to stand alone as external attempts at proof which, of course, invariably fail.[17] ... theology's proper task we find is the grammar of the faith.[18]

Phillips is effectively claiming that if statements such as those made about religion or morality are not empirical statements (as they are not verifiable), then they are only grammatical statements. He would take issue with the word 'only' because he is passionate in his conviction of the importance, meaning, depth and profundity or religious discourse, and the word 'only' can imply a diminution of the value of religious language. However, the sense in which I am accusing him of saying that language is 'only' grammatical is in the sense that Phillips rejects the idea of any ontological referent and, as the above debate with Lindbeck makes clear, he holds strongly to this view. He accuses Lindbeck of not being able to give any content to the claim that there is an ontological commitment involved in religious language. Such a content can easily be given, however. It represents the realist claim that theological language is true if and only if it successfully refers and the reference is not simply to a reality found within the believing community but goes beyond this to a substance. Phillips says:

> Consider two uses of 'This is red'. In the first, we are offering a description of a particular object. Someone has asked us what colour it is and we reply 'This is red'. But in the second use of 'This is red' nothing is being described. Rather, we are being given the rule for the use of the word 'red'. It seems to me that theological or doctrinal statements are often of the second form. They give us rules for the use of the word 'God' ... If, then, the doctrine is opposed and another proposed, the conflict in question is itself a grammatical conflict, not a factual conflict within an already agreed grammar ... God is love' may mislead us into thinking that it is a descriptive statement rather than a rule for the use of the word 'God'.[19]

Phillips' claim, however, that 'God is love' is not a descriptive statement is a denial of the central feature of religious belief. Religious faith *does* consider this to be a descriptive statement which successfully refers to the creator God. As such it may, of course, be false, which is part of the nature of a realist claim. Religious claims go far beyond mere grammatical assertions. Theology, says Phillips, answers the question 'What is Christianity?', but:

> ... it tells us the answer by giving us the order and priorities, the structure and morphology of the Christian faith. It does this by placing the big words, like MAN, GOD, JESUS, WORLD, in such a sequence and context that their use becomes ruled for us. And if we begin to use words like that, with the appropriate zest and pathos, then we, too, become Godly as those earlier believers were.[20]

The early believers did not simply accept the rules of linguistic usage for God-talk; they believed they were successfully referring to the God who created and sustains the world. Phillips seems to consider that the alternatives are either to assert that God's existence can be established by reason (by metaphysics) or to adopt his anti-realistic perspective. This, however, is simply false.

> ... If theologians are confronted by wholesale attacks on the metaphysical views on which they think religious belief depends, they will search desperately for alternative metaphysical views. As we have already suggested, there is something comic in the way theologians have hopped from one metaphysical view to another. What they will not admit, any more than their philosophic counterparts, is that when a metaphysical view fails, it need not be replaced by another one.[21]

To say that there are no proofs for the truth of realist religious truth claims is NOT the same as saying that these claims cannot be true in a realist sense. This is where faith comes in, the faith that affirms a commitment to a reality that cannot be proved and that may be mistaken.

William James, the American philosopher and psychologist, was challenged by a theology student who said that 'Philosophy is like a blind man in a dark cellar, looking for a black cat which isn't there'. 'Yes', replied James, 'and the difference between theology and philosophy is that theology finds the cat'. There is no proof that there is a cat in the cellar. Theology is sure it has found it, many philosophers deny that a cat exists because the evidence for it is ambiguous, and others hold that there may be a cat in the cellar and lack of proof is not proof that the cat does not exist.

Both Kierkegaard and Wittgenstein recognised this. Wittgenstein was clear that there are no provable foundations for language — we are educated into a form of life. Religious believers are those who stake their lives on certain claims made within a form of life which may or may not be true, but whether they are true or not depends on a state of affairs that is independent on the language game through which they are described.

A perspicuous understanding involves the individual realising how language works, that there are no foundations for language that we are educated into forms of life which depend on culture and the community in which we live. Once we see these things, then many former philosophical 'puzzles' will simply disappear. However, this is not the same as saying that religion and morality are just a language game, just a story we tell ourselves. All human beings have is the language with which they communicate, with which they talk of love and death, science and despair, and through which they try to stammer after the transcendent. Some stake their lives on claims made through language (how else can such claims be made?), on claims that cannot be proved. This does not mean that they can be dismissed, but it does mean that they must understand the need for humility and ambiguity and refuse to judge others because their own claims could be wrong.

THE SUFIS

Sufism has a considerable history, predating Islam. It is difficult to provide an accurate description of it and in a way it defies characterisation. In Western terms, Aesop's Fables (sixth century BC) may give an insight into Sufi methods or teaching of the Sufi masters which are often given by way of fable and parable. That which seems to be the case is often not. The Sufis are masters of indirect communication and readily appreciated that their words and teachings often fall on deaf ears. Indeed when people come to a Sufi master for instruction, the master is more likely than not to send them away because they are deemed incapable of receiving the teaching, at least in their present state.

Sufis have been among the foremost philosophers of the last thousand years, while recognising that reason and philosophy are but partial and limited ways to truth. Human beings, Sufis consider, have been conditioned and indoctrinated by their upbringing and culture, and breaking through this conditioning may be the most difficult task of all. The parallel to Kierkegaard seeking to indirectly communicate Christianity into a country that thinks it is Christian is obvious. Sufis also have a suspicion of institutional religion and of clerics, and they believe that each individual has to tread the path for themselves.

Sufism is about transformation of the self, helping someone to become a new individual. This means stripping away the laziness,

self-indulgence and complacency with which most people are content, and calling individuals to what they are capable of becoming.
The Sufis do not follow the path to truth in hope of a reward or
out of fear of punishment. To illustrate, Mohammed al-Ghazali, the
eleventh-century Islamic philosopher, quoted a story about Jesus.
Jesus passed several groups of people. Most were miserable because
they feared hell or hoped for heaven. Finally he came to one group
whose faces shone with joy. When he asked them why this was the
case, they answered: 'The Spirit of Truth. We have seen Reality and
this has made us oblivious of lesser goals.'[1]

The Sufis state that there is a form of knowledge which can be
achieved by human beings which is of a different order to traditional
philosophy, as adulthood is to infancy. al-Ghazali said:

> ... a child has no real knowledge of the attainments of an adult. An
> ordinary adult cannot understand the attainments of a learned man.
> In the same way, a learned man cannot understand the experiences
> of enlightened saints or Sufis.[2]

The same point was made in a book of Sufi teachings by Hazrat
Khan:

> The first stage in the awakening of the soul is a feeling. 'Is there not
> something else that I could know?' He feels dissatisfied with all he
> knows, with all the knowledge he may have from science, art, philos-
> ophy or literature. He comes to a stage where he feels, 'There is
> something else I must know that books, dogmas and beliefs cannot
> teach, something higher and greater than words can explain. This is
> what I want to know.'[3]

This is not a concept which would commend itself to the modern
day philosopher, still less the theologian, although it might well
have been recognised by St Paul who said that the preaching of
Christianity would be 'foolishness' to many who heard it. This is not
a new problem. In the eleventh century Mohammed al-Ghazali told
the philosophers of his time that their way of knowing things was
inferior to the knowledge gained through Sufi mystical methods.
They made him their hero, and their successors still teach his interpretations as orthodox Islam, in spite of al-Ghazali stating that the
whole academic way of approaching knowledge is insufficient and
inferior to real knowledge. This presents a real problem. If there
really is a form of knowledge, a type of truth, that goes beyond that
which can be verified, that which can be taught in books or learnt

from a lecturer, then a different understanding of truth than the one normally adopted is required.

Rumi, the great Sufi mystic and poet, told his audiences that like a good host he gave them poetry because they demanded it, providing what was asked for. Poetry, he considered, provided insights into truth that were not available elsewhere, because poetry could show truth in a way that academic philosophy failed to do. However, in spite of the superiority of poetry over philosophy, he maintained that poetry was of little account compared with the possibility of the high development of the individual who follows the mystical way. Sufis claim that some people do not *want* the knowledge that Sufis aim to impart; they really seek only their own satisfactions within their own system of thinking, within the comfort zone of their own community. Sufi masters such as Rumi insist, however, that even a short time in the presence of the Friends (the Sufis) is better that a hundred years of sincere obedient dedication to some religious system.

Ibn al-Arabi was born in 1165 and became a Sufi at the age of twenty. He was one of the greatest Sufi philosophers and mystics. He said:

> The Sufi must act and speak in a manner which takes into consideration the understanding, limitations and dominant concealed prejudices of his audience.[4]

This is precisely what Kierkegaard did. He used indirect communication to try to get people to 'see' truth, albeit a truth that reason cannot prove. Mohammed did not claim that Islam was a new religion. Rather, it was the culmination of a monotheistic tradition which started with the early Fathers such as Abraham, continued in the Israelite tradition through Moses and was then continued in the Christian tradition and Jesus. Islam insists that truth has been available at all times at specific stages. Prophets are sent by God to particular people at stages in their history — prophets include not only the great figures of the Hebrew tradition but also messengers sent by God to other nations. Islam claims that human beings continually introduced distortions into the revelations of God and, therefore, the Koran had to be dictated to provide a final revelation. Yet, it is too easy for the Koran, or any other book, to become ossified and 'dead' so that it fails to capture the spirit involved. Sufis have always been aware of this. There have been times when prominent

Sufis have been under suspicion and attack for not being sufficient-ly orthodox Muslims. Ibn al-Arabi himself was denounced in Cairo by the theologians who stirred up such a reaction against him that his life was threatened. This is not, perhaps, surprising as in every religious tradition the mystical part tends to challenge those whose religion is bound by narrow doctrinal frameworks.

One of the main reasons that Sufism is so poorly understood in the West is that it is a *way*, a way of transforming an individual. It is not a doctrine or a religion in the conventional sense, and anyone seeking to study it from outside will fail to comprehend it. Sufism involves a passionate search for truth in which all material concerns are put into second place, but it is a truth that transcends normal categories and which is highly subjective. It involves calling human beings to that of which they are individually capable, but this is a path that each individual has to choose for themselves. It simply is not possible to buy a couple of books about Sufism, read them and then claim to have understood what it is to be a Sufi. The only per-son who will really understand something of what Sufism involves is the person who tries to follow the Sufi way. This way is difficult, it involves a total transformation of the self and all the normal priori-ties of life, and it involves living in a new way. It is not surprising then that few are willing to take this path.

Sufism is a progressive and life-long journey. The fables that contain Sufi teachings are meant to challenge the perceptions and understanding of those who hear them. One set of these fables are the Nasrudin stories. Nasrudin probably did not exist, but the sto-ries about him nevertheless disclose truths. One story is as follows. A king was complaining to Nasrudin that his subjects were untruth-ful. Nasrudin replied:

> Majesty, there is truth and truth. People must practise real truth before they can use relative truth. They always try the other way round. The result is that they take liberties with their man-made truth, because they know instinctively that it is only an invention.

The king thought that this was too complicated because he believed that something was either true or false. He decided to make people tell the truth and by so doing instil in them the habit of truthful-ness. He therefore set up gallows at the entrance to his town and everyone entering had to answer a question as they came in. Nasrudin was the first to come in, and the captain of the guard asked him: 'Where are you going? Tell the truth — the alternative is death by hanging.' Nasrudin replied: 'I am going to be hung on the gallows.' 'I don't believe you', said the captain. 'Then hang me', said Nasrudin. The captain realised, of course, that if he hung him then he would have hung a truthful man.[5]

The Sufi point is that what is good or bad often depends on individual or group criteria and a great deal depends on perspective. The point is made by another story about Nasrudin. He was once invited to a bear hunt by a king who liked him to go on such hunts. Nasrudin was very frightened but he had to go. When he returned to his village in the evening, his friends asked him: 'How did the hunt go?' 'Very well', replied Nasrudin. 'How many bears did you see?' asked his friends. 'None', replied Nasrudin. 'How could the hunt have gone marvellously then?' his friends asked. Nasrudin replied: 'If you are hunting bears, and when you are me, seeing no bears at all is a marvellous experience.'[6]

The Sufi mystics, like the mystics within other great religious traditions, seek truth but not through philosophy or theology. William James maintained that there are four marks of mystical experience, two of these being: that mystical experiences are passive; and that they have a noetic quality. In other words the mystic is a passive recipient of such experiences and these experiences provide knowledge. This knowledge, in turn, mystics claim, provides access to a type of truth that is not available elsewhere. Sufi mystics seek to live this Truth.

19

VACLAV HAVEL AND LIVING THE TRUTH

LIVING IN THE TRUTH

Vaclav Havel, poet, philosopher, playwright, former President of the Czech Republic, was imprisoned for four years by the Communist Government. He was allowed to write one letter a week to his wife, Olga. On 7 January 1980 he wrote about a Prague greengrocer who ran a small shop. In the shop window he placed a sign saying 'Workers of the World Unite'. No-one looking at the shop window took any notice of the sign, for they had similar signs in their shops and offices, which were delivered every week. Certainly the people looking at the shop window noticed if there were any tomatoes or other fruit and whether they were fresh, but the sign was ignored. What, then, was the function of the sign? It was put there by the greengrocer to say, 'I will be a loyal citizen. I will conform to the system, I will not rock the boat.' The reward for the greengrocer was his job, a small flat, being allowed to send his son to college, and a week's holiday each year in Bulgaria. One day, however, something in the greengrocer snaps. He decides to take down the sign and to stand for what he believes. He decides to 'live in the Truth' (as Havel put it). For Havel, living in the Truth is not to live by one's own truth, but to be responsible to something ultimate, beyond one's psyche, one's community or society. Havel never actually identified this Unknown with God, but his position is very similar to Kierkegaard who also described God as the

Unknown. Truth is not relative. If one achieves purity of heart, if one purges one's motives such as selfishness, fear and hope for reward, one may come to live in the Truth. This, for Havel and Kierkegaard, is not a truth that is created but a truth grounded in a relationship with the Unknown Other which some call God. It is a truth that is lived on a day-to-day basis. True religion is not a matter of ceremonies or words; it is a matter of living in the truth of a relationship.

There is a human need to belong, to have the assurance of being part of a group and being reassured by the group that one is right. This naturally leads to anti-realism or to constructivism in psychology. There is a yearning to find a group to which one can conform and to give up any sense of being an individual precisely because this is too lonely, too isolating. Dostoyevsky put it like this in *Crime and Punishment*:

> There is nothing a free man is so anxious to do as to find something to worship. But it must be something unquestionable, that all men agree can be worshipped communally. For the great concern of these miserable creatures is not that every individual should find something to worship that he personally considers worthy of worship, but that they should find something in which they can all believe and which they can all worship in common. It is essential that it should be in common. And it is precisely that requirement of shared worship that has been the principal source of suffering for individual man and the human race since the beginning of history. In their efforts to impose universal worship, men have unsheathed their swords and killed one another.

Crusades, holy wars and the attempt by religious groups to impose their certainties on others and secure a communal approach to truth are the enemies of any true understanding of religion because they substitute conformity and the comfort zone for individual struggle and commitment. This process is also at work in politics and in history, even though some historians deny this.

A popular fiction has grown regarding the history of Scotland, namely that on Bonnie Prince Charlie's return all the Highland clans, except the traitor Campbells, rose immediately in support of him; that the final defeat of the Scots at Culloden was the result of the victory of an English war machine against the gallant Scots. This is simply not true, however. Sir Walter Scott's gifted story telling must take a large measure of blame for this. Sir Walter Scott produced a romanticised and false picture of history which has become accepted by many as orthodoxy.[1] This does not mean that it is true, for fantasy remains fantasy even if it is widely believed. Today, this is more important than ever with political forces seeking to mould history to suit their own agenda. This has happened in many countries occupied by colonial powers when the rich oral history of the native peoples has been suppressed by the history of the colonialists. Post-modernists are right to emphasise the power involved in such movements, but are mistaken in claiming there is no truth to be sought or that it is not possible to move closer to, or further away from, a truthful understanding.

In Havel's own country, Czechoslovakia, the communists came to power by a coup in 1949. Their excuse was that, in free elections, some 37 per cent of the population had voted Communist. One of the first things the new government did was to get rid of the old history books and substitute them with a new history. The Communist Party became dominant as it conferred the right to belong, the alternative being an isolation that precluded the individual from almost all forms of activity and very probably involved arrest and imprisonment. New communal rituals were substituted for the old. Thus new communist marriage celebrations replaced old Christian rites. Baptism was replaced by a ceremony of 'welcoming new citizens to life'. People quickly learned that failure to participate in the communal vision brought swift and effective punishment. Anyone who stood out lost their job, accommodation and much else. It became simply foolish to deny the reality and reject the imposed view.

Naturally, under this sort of regime, philosophers, writers, artists and intellectuals were treated with the gravest suspicion because they were most likely to be willing to think for themselves and to refuse to conform. These individuals had to be eliminated or at least forced to comply because they used their imagination. They had to be 're-educated' or, in the case of Pol Pot's regime in Cambodia, killed. Being an individual was seen as a crime. (The same happened in Maoist China and in Marxist Russia — and the same happens in fundamentalist Shia or Sunni Islam or in sections of the Christian Church today.) If anyone stood up against these systems they were shunned and condemned by their fellows. This was partly due to cowardice because the consequences of taking a stand were perceived as being too great. To prevent the lie entering society by standing on the side of truth can mean risking one's life, one's family and one's livelihood. Because the majority had accepted the communal truth, rejection of this agreed truth was seen as subversive and rebellious. If the majority is willing to live with an imposed view of truth and if this view is then challenged, this challenge is likely to be seen as threatening. Persecution is, therefore, the means used by those in power and by the majority to maintain the fiction by which they live.

Havel claimed that the Communist Government and other autocratic systems maintained their power by the force of a lie — precisely the opposite of any idea of truth:

> Because the regime is captive to its own lies, it must falsify everything. It falsifies the past. It falsifies the present and it falsifies the future. It falsifies statistics. It pretends not to possess an omnipotent and unprincipled police apparatus. It pretends to respect human rights. It pretends to fear nothing. It pretends to pretend nothing.

> Individuals need not believe all these mystifications, but they must behave as though they did, or they must at least tolerate them in silence, or get along well with those who work with them. For this reason, however, they must live within a lie. They need not escape the lie. It is enough for them to have accepted their life with it and in it. For by this very fact, individuals confirm the system, fulfil the system, make the system, are the system.

We have here a clear example of truth as a construct which people must either believe or at least tacitly accept. Havel makes clear, however, that this construct, and the truths that are accepted within it, are a lie. They fail to represent an accurate vision of the world. It is to the construct that Havel's greengrocer conforms because the alternative seems impossible — the ordinary person appears impotent in the face of the power of the state or the group. It is this conclusion that Havel wishes to reject.

The greengrocer places his 'Workers of the World Unite' notice in the window as a sign of his submission, his willingness to obey the system, his acceptance of the need to acquiesce. It appears that the greengrocer is impotent, but this is precisely what Havel challenges. Why, after all, does the system need the greengrocer's submission? The very fact that his submission is important shows that he is powerful rather than powerless. Havel spells the point out:

> We have seen that the real meaning of the greengrocer's slogan has nothing to do with what the text of the slogan actually says. Even so, the real meaning is quite clear and generally comprehensible because the code is so familiar: the greengrocer declares his loyalty in the only

way the regime is capable of hearing; that is, by accepting the pre-scribed ritual, by accepting appearances as reality, by accepting the given rules of the game, thus making it possible for the game to go on, for it to exist in the first place.

Thus the sign (Workers of the World Unite) helps the greengrocer to conceal from himself the low foundations of his obedience, at the same time concealing the low foundations of power. It hides them behind the facade of something high. And that something is ideology.

IDEOLOGY AND LIVING A LIE

Ideology produces truths to live by. Ideology is the vehicle by which anti-realism proclaims the truths it has created, just as propaganda is the means by which ideology is disseminated. Individual truths are suppressed beneath an enforced ideology, and conformity is ensured by the exercise of power and by the willingness of those in authority to exclude those who dissent.

Crowds at major ceremonies such as communist parades confirm the strength and power of the system. These attendances occur because they are compulsory or at least are strongly encouraged. These are the rituals of the system and it is by performing rituals, whether putting up a sign or attending a parade, that individuals indicate their obedience. It *matters* that people attend and conform, and it is here that the power of individuals lies, the power of weakness which is in fact strength. Because obedience matters, individuals have the choice not to obey. Certainly rebellion against established orthodoxy may carry uncomfortable consequences, but this is not an effective argument. Failure to obey the Nazis undoubtedly carried severe penalties, even death, but this does not mean that obedience was right.

Havel reaches a much more radical conclusion, namely that if individuals have the power to refuse to accept the prevailing ideology, then they cannot escape responsibility if they do accept the ideology. Their failure to stand out against a system is itself a moral failure. This is a surprising and challenging conclusion. It means that the comfort zone, belonging to a group, conforming to generally accepted ethical and social norms may represent a moral failure. Conforming to the status quo is a moral act and cannot be excused. There have been too many times throughout history when men and women have done exactly that.

The steps in Havel's argument are effectively:

1. Totalitarian systems, whether these are political, institutional, corporate or ecclesiastical impose their constructed views of truth by means of ideology, mythical stories and ritual. This imposition is backed by a system of organised violence (which may or may not be physical) and power.

2. Compliance, obedience and a willingness to participate in the system matter as these are the means by which the system and its controllers maintain power and influence. The world of appearance is maintained in existence by the compliance of the majority.

3. The system will, therefore, use whatever means is necessary to enforce compliance, notably exclusion with various penalties. This is where the real struggle takes places — between a few individuals who refused to conform and the power of the institution.

4. In spite of the power of the system, individuals have the ability to refuse to comply. This is Havel's realist claim: there is ultimate truth to which the individual must be responsible.

5. Because individuals can refuse to comply, they are culpable if they fail to stand up against the system and instead conform in the interests of their own security.

6. This means that each individual must take responsibility for living in the Truth, responsible to an ultimate Truth which goes beyond the individual psyche or community. This responsibility cannot be avoided by conformity to the institution or community since conformity is itself a moral choice. Religious people will see this ultimate Truth as resting in God, whereas non-religious people may speak in other, possibly Platonic, terms.

7. Failure to live in the Truth is a moral failure for which individuals must account.

Notice that the first step includes ecclesiastical systems together with political and corporate systems. All may be used because it is through compliance that unity and security are found. In this sense,

Nietzsche was right to recognise the widespread existence of power relationships between human beings. However, it may be precisely in resisting this power that truthfulness may lie. Living in the Truth may mean resisting the power of evil found within structures through which it operates. All the greengrocer's friends would have conformed and would have found it almost inexplicable that he could have staked his life on standing out and achieving, apparently, nothing. Almost all of them would have rejected him as the 'outsider' on whom society turns its back.

Living in the Truth is very different from accepting religious or moral truths laid down by any group. As with other systems, to live in the Truth may require the individual to stand against the religious group to which he or she belongs and to which primary loyalty may otherwise be given. This can create real tension for individuals who belong to such groups. They may well seek to deceive themselves and to suppress questioning because they realise that once they allow themselves to recognise a claim to truth, they will find themselves in an intolerable position. Some examples may illustrate this problem:

1. A young Nazi joined the Waffen SS in 1942 and gave an oath of loyalty to the Feurher. If he then came to consider that Hitler was wrong, few would doubt that he had a moral duty to reject Hitler (in spite of his oath) and to 'live in the Truth' even though this may well have cost him his life.

2. A young US airman who joined up to fight in Vietnam took an oath of loyalty to his country and president and then felt that, in order to live in the Truth, he had to disobey the order to slaughter innocent Vietnamese.

3. A married woman swore fidelity and lifelong commitment to her husband. She then found he was a wife-beater who suppressed her very person and who made her life hell. He also refused to allow their children to have a religious education even thought she considered that providing children with the option to take a religious perspective seriously was important. She might decide that 'living in the Truth' meant recognising that the marriage was at an end and she should leave.

4. A man in Ghana who married three wives and then became a

Christian might then find that he felt compelled to renounce two of the wives.

Truth, then, can come into conflict with a vow of obedience. Which will have primacy? The Kotzker, Kierkegaard, Wittgenstein and Havel all maintain that it is truth that must always be first.

Religious people, like people in every other way of life, will often have a strong motivation to deceive themselves and to convince themselves that their group has the Truth. Any appeal beyond the group can be seen as 'sinful', wicked and to be resisted. Such individuals will be threatened by philosophy or by independent thought because they see the danger that this might undermine their own cherished beliefs. Often those who are most violently opposed to a position are those who are personally most threatened by it. We may well ask why this is the case. It may be that the fierceness of their opposition is a means to ensure that they do not have to face their own uncertainties about the truth of their position. Fundamentalism is often a manifestation of a fear of confronting truth or ambiguity. It is a means of self-protection. Havel claims that there is a moral dimension to this which cannot be avoided.

20

FEAR AND FREEDOM

THE FEAR OF TRUTH

Fear is an insufficiently acknowledged human emotion that is closely linked to truth. To seek truth may mean overcoming the fear that one's own certainties and most cherished convictions may be wrong or the fear of facing the consequences of a claim to truth. Fear may prevent an individual seeking to 'know themselves' because it is too painful. Many who are within long-term, committed relationships may be fearful of looking honestly at these relationships. Human beings are experts at running away from truth and will use every means to avoid facing it. Once an individual stands on the side of truth, the values accepted by society and the group that individual inhabits may have to be challenged and rejected. The price to be paid for any individual who does this may be high. In everyday examples, facing truth may mean that one rejects a religious group that one has accepted for all one's life, that one rejects the values of a business by whom one is employed or a political party which one has served.

Fear also insulates individuals from confronting the truth about themselves. Human beings are complex and we are affected by many factors. Confronting truth about ourselves may be painful and difficult. The more we learn about the human genome, the more it may become apparent that many of our behavioural trends are genetically determined. We carry within us the genes that will decide what diseases and ailments may come to us and even when it is likely that we will die. The truth about our upbringing and background may directly affect our sexuality and our ability to form relationships. The mistakes we have made in the past leave a legacy which may be difficult to overcome. Behavioural patterns may have become established and set, and confronting the truth about these may be difficult. Self-knowledge is, as Apollo's priests recognised, a central part of wisdom, but is a painful journey and one which we never complete.

Living in the Truth may mean rejecting family and friends and standing alone on the side of Truth against what appears to be the entire world. The loneliness of this path cannot be emphasised strongly enough. Havel's greengrocer was isolated from his customers, friends and family, Francis of Assisi rejected his family and their whole way of life, and Trevor Huddleston, Nelson Mandela and Vaclav Havel in different ways confronted the might of the society in which they lived and paid a heavy price for so doing. But this should come as no surprise. Those who wish to live in the Truth have always been a very small minority, outsiders who at times must have wondered if they were mad or deceived. Even Prophet Elijah, having stood firmly against King Ahab and his wife Jezebel in the service of Truth, was forced to flee for his life. He ended up alone, in a cave, hunted like a wild animal and feeling fundamentally isolated. He said to God:

'I alone am left, and they seek to take my life.'
Then God asks him, as if it were not obvious:
'Elijah, why are you here?'
Elijah replies: 'I have been most zealous for the Lord, the God of hosts. But the Israelites have forsaken your covenant, torn down your altars, and put your prophets to the sword. I alone am left, and they seek to take my life.'[1]

Far from offering safe refuge, God commands Elijah to go and anoint two new kings of Aram and Israel and a new prophet who will take his work forward, Elisha. God, however, also offers Elijah a word of comfort saying that there are still seven thousand men in Israel who remain faithful. So it is with truth today. Truth has become a dirty word, spat on and derided, mocked and denigrated, but still there are many who, with passion and integrity, seek to follow Truth and to be faithful to it no matter what the personal cost. The personal cost is not just measured in external but also in internal terms.

Shakespeare's *Hamlet* recognised this. The play is about Hamlet wrestling with the nature of truth: the nature of the apparition of his dead father, the truth of who killed his father and who he is as a human being. *Hamlet* raises issues that are as relevant to us today as they were to those who first saw the play. The key issues are:

1. What is Man?
2. What should I be?
3. What should I do?

These issues go to the heart of the human condition. They depend on a search for truth, a search on which Hamlet embarks. However, Hamlet verges on madness because he is on the very edge, in fear of himself and his search for truth and understanding. The line between madness and integrity may be a narrow one, but one that people have to walk today.

The world of Hamlet[2] is one of chaos and anxiety, an 'unweeded garden' as Hamlet calls it. Everyone spies on everyone else, everyone is looking over their shoulder, and nothing is certain. Even the request given to him by his father's ghost ('this thing', 'this dreaded sight', 'a spirit of heaven and goblin damned') is full of ambiguity. He is not sure whether the ghost is good or evil. Hamlet does not know whether he is confronted with a figment of his imagination or with something real. We are back to the realism and anti-realism question. Has Hamlet created his father's ghost in his psyche or is there really a transcendent order from which his father can appear to him? He does not know and his uncertainty tortures him.

The idea of the play is how Man, whom Hamlet represents, works out his destiny in the light of knowing that he lives between two worlds, the world of the beast and of the angel. Supernaturalism and naturalism are always contrasted. Polonious is eaten by worms, and yet, man is noble in reason and infinite in faculty. *Hamlet* is a play about ambiguity and about the human condition, about seeking to find a way when one is trying to be good and truthful in a world where truth is elusive and ambiguous.

Hamlet does not see his task, to avenge his father's murder, as being a matter of ethics. After all, revenge morality, as seen in the case of Laertes, was regarded as honourable. So, he has no real conscience about this. However, Hamlet worries about why he should have to be the 'scourge and minister' for heaven's justice. The play shows him working out his place in the wider scheme of things. He is wrestling with a truthful understanding of the human condition and he is willing to live with the fear to which this gives rise. He could simply conform as everyone around him wishes him to do, but the loss of his integrity is too high a price to pay.

Some post-modernists would hold that there is no intrinsic difference in value between Shakespeare and television soap operas like *Home and Away* or *Eastenders*. However, this is simply perverse. Shakespeare's genius is to show us insights into the human condition which are the result of unique natural ability and a huge emotional and intellectual investment. Their relevance has been shown by the appeal Shakespeare's works have had over the centuries in different cultures around the world and by their relevance to constantly changing conditions and times. Soap operas, by contrast, are written for financial reward and are essentially ephemeral. Great writers have often challenged the system by revealing things about the culture in which they lived, and sometimes the result has been persecution and imprisonment. The writers of soap operas face no such challenges. Great literature confronts us with insights into truth, into what it is to be human. These insights can and should challenge us, but all too rarely do we allow them to disturb the comfort of our lives. To stand for the value of great literature, art or music is often to be confronted by amused resignation or indifference or by downright rejection.

Modern psychology, with its emphasis on living successfully in the world, may be a denial of the search for truth in favour of a way of living that leads to conformity and the comfort zone. Hamlet and the great thinkers of the past lay firmly outside this zone. Once truth is denied, then an essential element of what it is to be human dies with it as well and we are left with mediocrity. However, the stand against mediocrity is to stand against the crowd, and most people are too fearful to do this.

Living in fear of truth and living in fear of God are very similar, both involving a refusal to compromise, a willingness to stand for something higher than is accepted by society or community. The fear of God is constantly referred to in the Hebrew and Christian scriptures. The wicked are described as those who have no fear of God;[3] those who fear God need nothing else beside, it is better than either health or wealth;[4] holiness is found through the fear of God;[5] and justice is found in those who rule in the fear of God.[6] Most clearly stated, however, is the link between the fear of God and wisdom:

- 'The fear of the Lord is the beginning of wisdom; prudent are all who live by it.' (Psalm 111:10)
- 'The beginning of wisdom is the fear of the Lord, and knowledge of the Holy One is understanding.' (Proverbs 9:10)
- 'The beginning of wisdom is fear of the Lord.' (Sirach 1:12)

If 'The Lord' and God are one and the same and if the central divine attribute is truth, then the picture becomes clear. To live in the Truth, to be fearful above all else of living a life that departs from the Truth, no matter what the cost and the pain to oneself or to others, is the highest form of wisdom. Yet there is almost nothing that human beings will not do to avoid this, because what is feared is not truth but a lack of comfort, a feeling of rejection or exclusion, losing one's job or the approval of one's friends or family, or suffering in material terms.

If fear is directed at one's own safety or the preservation of one's material possessions, reputation or even family, then this is likely to be destructive and lead to a loss of integrity. Such fear needs to be faced and overcome whatever the cost may be. There is an issue of personal integrity or 'selfhood' here which is at the heart of the debate. The claim is that if one loses one's 'self', one will have lost the most precious thing of all.

Fear of loss of external things starts in the classroom, and many young people live in constant fear of not being accepted, not being seen to be the same as their peers. 'Peer group pressure' is a direct result of fear of being an individual because this is too costly. Sadly our schools often fail young people in this area by not valuing difference. There are clear ideas within the culture of most schools as to what constitutes success and acceptability, and any attempt at individuality tends to be quickly suppressed. Fear is an excellent spur to suppress freedom.

FREEDOM AND TRUTH

Living in the Truth is, for Vaclav Havel, more important than knowing the Truth. When Havel himself was imprisoned, he was an embarrassment because he was well known as a poet, philosopher and playwright. First the authorities tried to stop his works being performed, then they tried to intimidate him, then they imprisoned him. He refused to compromise and his willingness to stand against the authorities made him an embarrassment. He was told by the authorities that if he would ask for a pardon he would be released. If he would accept an invitation to lecture in the United States he would be allowed to leave the country. However, he refused as this would have been a compromise. Havel sought a true freedom by being willing to go to gaol. Richard Lovelace, the English poet, made the same point:

> Stone walls do not a prison make,
> Nor iron bars a cage;
> Minds innocent and quiet
> take that for a hermitage.
> If I have freedom in my soul,
> And in my love am free;
> Angels alone that dwell above
> Enjoy such liberty.[7]

Freedom means much more than being out of prison. Most people are constrained by the dull compulsions of everyday life. They imprison themselves within systems, by ambitions, money and possessions, or sometimes by marriage and family. Most people gladly abandon themselves to these chains. In Czechoslovakia the people who were most free were those in prison, while the party officials and those who had to live within the system (like the greengrocer) were the most constrained. In the West today most people think that they are free but in fact their freedom is massively constrained by chains that bind them and take away their freedom to live in the Truth.

Individuals wish to surrender their freedom, which is why fundamentalism is so appealing to people who want nothing more than to be told what to believe. They do not want to think, they do not want to wrestle, and they seek security and certainty because this is comfortable. Outside the comfort zone everything is unsure, unclear and ambiguous. Living in the Truth involves struggle and uncertainty. It means renouncing the comfort of possessions and ambitions as the highest goal for which one aims and instead substituting a commitment to something higher and more significant which is not easily grasped.

Havel said that after he was made President of the newly formed Czech Republic, the inability of individuals to trust themselves, their fear of responsibility, was one of the worst scars the forty-five years of communism had inflicted upon a once-free people. The Czechs and Slovaks, he said, had passed through a dark tunnel, at the end of which there was the light of freedom. Unexpectedly they had passed through prison gates and had found themselves in a square. They were now free and they did not know where to go. When they were in prison, they knew where the walls were, they knew exactly where they would bump their heads and get a bloody nose. Now a whole people were calling for new walls, new boundaries and to be told what to do. They could not handle the gift of freedom.

This can, perhaps, be illustrated by reference to the institutional Catholic Church. I have the highest possible regard for this Church and many of my closest friends have devoted their lives to its service. However, in the area of truth and freedom its record is blemished — in spite of the commitment of many of its greatest scholars to the search for truth. In using it as an example, I am conscious that many other churches and religions have a far worse record. However, it is because of the high regard and affection I have for the Catholic Church and the depth of its intellectual heritage that it seems fitting to recognise that, when it comes to claims to truth, its own record is ambiguous at best.

Germain Grisez, one of the foremost conservative Catholic moral theologians, said:

> We believe that our Lord teaches in and through the Church and gives us the word of the Father. Hence, our submission to the Church's teaching is not submission to mere human opinions, but to the very word of God.[8]

Grisez claimed that a faithful Catholic is not in a position to think that any moral doctrine proposed by the Pope or the Magisterium is wrong unless he or she can appeal either to Scripture or to previous teachings of the Magisterium. However, even these limited exceptions hardly apply to Papal teaching:

In the case of Papal teaching, however, there is little chance of its being undercut by a superior theological source.[9]

Grisez maintains that even if one is wrong in following Church teaching, one would not be responsible for being wrong, since to follow Church teaching would be equivalent to following one's conscience.

Bernard Hoose, one of the leading international liberal Catholic moral theologians, in his book *Received Wisdom*[10] rejects this approach and he gives three examples:

1. For many years the 'divine right of kings' was maintained. Any resistance to the king was considered to be a sin and to ensure damnation. The king was accountable to God alone and non-resistance and passive obedience to the monarch was enjoined by the law of God.[11] This position would no longer be accepted.

2. Leo X condemned Martin Luther for saying that burning heretics at the stake was against the will of God. It is true that in 1966, the Second Vatican Council excluded the burning of heretics, but surely, Hoose says, even before this many ordinary Christians had already excluded this even if Pope Leo's teaching was still officially the Magisterium's position. Pope Leo was mistaken.

3. Grisez acknowledges that Scripture could be used as a criterion to judge pronouncements by the Magisterium, but the Magisterium has tried to control the Bible and has suppressed and forcibly subdued those who opposed it. The Pontifical Biblical Commission made many errors, yet in 1907 Pope Pius X endorsed the Commission's decrees. These decrees forced obedience onto the faithful and a number of prominent scholars were excommunicated as a result. The Commission said, in 1906, that all Catholics had to acknowledge that Moses was 'substantially' the author of the first five books of the Bible. Hoose comments:

   I imagine that if any Catholic Biblical scholar made such an assertion today, he or she would be assumed by colleagues to be joking, ill, over-tired or drunk.[12]

Yet for nearly sixty years Catholic Biblical scholars were prevented from engaging in any really significant academic work. They were suppressed and forcibly controlled. Hoose gives as an example a Biblical scholar in the United States, Fr Henry Poels, who was called on to swear an oath which read:

I, Henry Poels, do promise, vow and swear upon God's Holy Gospels that I will sincerely accept and faithfully teach all the doctrines and conclusions that the Pontifical Commission has promulgated now and in the future.[13]

The Biblical Commission, the Magisterium and the Popes who supported their views for sixty years were mistaken.

4. For hundreds of years usury was an excommunicable offence. Now the lending of money at interest is permitted.

5. Many generations of Popes specifically sanctioned the persecution and oppression of the Jews. As one of many examples of decrees issued against the Jews, the First Lateran Council in 1215 promulgated a series of decrees affecting the Jewish community. Nearly 1500 Christian bishops and other leaders endorsed the decisions of Pope Innocent III. For instance, regarding clothing, the Council said:

It is decreed that henceforth Jews of both sexes will be distinguished from other peoples by their garments ... They will not show them-selves in public during Holy Week, for some among them on these days wear their finest garments and mock the Christian clad in mourning. Trespassers will be duly punished by the secular powers, in order that they no longer dare flout Christ in the presence of Christians.

Enforcement of these measures varied between countries. In France a circular badge of yellow cloth was worn. Later, in Nazi Germany, yellow Star of David had to be worn. The concentra-tion camps of Nazi Germany were not isolated instances; they were the culmination of continual oppression of the Jewish peo-ple by the Christian Church, with Popes, bishops and the Magisterium often taking the lead.

6. In 1210 and 1215 the Church condemned Aristotle's *Physics* and *Metaphysics*, and in 1228 Pope Gregory IX forbade contact with Greek philosophy. Within three hundred years, Aristotle's philoso-phy became the foundation stone for Catholic moral teaching. It has been argued by some that Pope Gregory and the Church degrees before him may well have been equally wrong in relying on Aristotle through the work of St Thomas Aquinas.

7. In 1616 the Pope made Galileo promise not to hold, teach or defend the ideas of Copernicus — that the Earth went round the Sun. In 1990 Pope John Paul II admitted that this was a mistake. A whole series of Popes and the Magisterium had been wrong.

8. The attitude to abortion has undergone huge changes in the life of the Church. Aquinas in 1265 followed Aristotle and maintained that foetuses received a soul at forty days in the case of males and ninety days in the case of females. He said that abortion before these dates was sinful because, like birth control, it frustrated the purpose of conception, but it was not murder because a soul was not present. In 1588, however, Pope Sixtus V effectively said that from the point of view of Church (Canon) Law and Secular Law, *any* abortion should be considered as murder. This decree met strong opposition, so Pope Gregory XIV returned to earlier laws, and the abortion of a foetus which had not received a soul and was considered to be 'animated' was no longer considered to be an act of murder. In 1869, Pope Pius IX pronounced the decree of excommunication on all those who procured abortion, whatever the age of the foetus. The Catholic Church today remains committed to the rejection of (almost) all forms of abortion, but the detail of the teaching and the understanding of the status of the embryo has changed.

9. Many Popes have blessed armies going to war and excommunicated those who opposed them. The Cardinal of Milan blessed Mussolini's tanks and aircraft as they set out to defeat the Ethiopians who had few arms besides camels and rifles. He said that the troops were bringing Catholicism to the heathen, even though the Ethiopians were largely Coptic Christians. Although some individual theologians have taught about Just War doctrines, these have rarely resulted in condemnation of major wars. The Magisterium did little to oppose Hitler in the Second World War, seeing the fascists as a bulwark against communism and helping some Nazi war criminals to escape after the war. The Church and the Popes specifically supported the Crusades.

10. The practice of paying for indulgences in order to be let off time in Purgatory was official Church policy for centuries. The reformers who rejected this approach were condemned and persecuted.

Some were burnt to death as heretics. The Church now acknowledges that these burnings were inappropriate. In 1998 the Pope once again emphasised the 'truth' about Purgatory and that by going on pilgrimages Catholics could get time off the period they would spend in Purgatory. The truth of such claims, at least in a realist sense, must be regarded as at best doubtful.

11. The Church rejected and condemned any attempt to translate the Bible into the vernacular, condemning, excommunicating and in some sense burning those who attempted the translations. The Church has now accepted translations.

12. Masturbation has been condemned in many Church documents as a mortal sin and, indeed, in the Middle Ages it was considered a worse sin than rape. This led to despair and suicide, yet few people today would take such a decree seriously. In recent documents the Church has recognised that there are many mitigating circumstances that would reduce the gravity of the sin.

I could go on with more examples but the basic point should now be clear. Any sense of history will indicate that Popes and the Magisterium of the Roman Catholic Church have been regularly and consistently wrong on some key issues. In 1968 the Pope ignored the strong majority view of the commission he had himself established to look at birth control. What is worse, it has been suggested that one of the central reasons for ignoring the majority view was that:

> The Roman Catholic Church could not change its teaching regarding the wrongness of such behaviour because it could not have erred so atrociously and for such a long time regarding so serious a matter which imposed heavy burdens on people.[14]

The strict rules the Pope imposed have caused untold sufferings to millions around the world who tried to be 'faithful Catholics'. Today, the policy is increasingly disregarded. Nevertheless, partly as a result of this policy, in many countries the birth rate is out of control.

It may, of course, be said that in the case of the Catholic Church these events are in the past. The problem is that this is not the case. The same tendency, in fact a reinforced tendency, has been imposed in the last ten years. First, a new oath was introduced on 1 March

1989, which all deacons now have to sign. The first part consists of the Creed, followed by:

I also firmly accept and hold each and everything definitively proposed by the Church concerning its teachings on faith and morals.

Moreover I adhere with religious submission of intellect and will to the teachings which either the Roman Pontiff or the College of Bishops enunciate in the exercise of their authentic teaching authority, even if they do not intend to proclaim these teachings as a definitive act.

This represents an unprecedented increase in the power of the Magisterium and those whom it appoints. It also ensures that only those who are willing to conform and declare an oath that they will give this assent will be ordained.

Canon 812 caused even more problems. It states:

It is necessary that those who teach theological disciplines in any institute of higher studies have a mandate from the competent ecclesiastical authority.

This did not originate in the Second Vatican Council in 1965, nor in the 1917 Code of Canon Law (which was in force until 1993), but in Germany in 1884 when the hierarchy was struggling to regain control over the teaching of religion in newly secularised schools. This canon has no history so it cannot be interpreted from an historical context. This has raised major protests from many academic institutions on the grounds of limitation of academic freedom and theological investigation, and conflicts with teachers unions and government regulations. Canon 18 directs that wherever a law restricts the free exercise of a right it should be interpreted strictly. This code is now firmly in place although some Archdioceses choose not to implement it fully. Archbishop George Pell in the Melbourne Archdiocese is, however, one of many who are taking a highly conservative line and thereby influencing the freedom of education in schools under his control in the interests of ensuring that young people receive only 'the truth'.

In 1994 all Catholic teachers in Catholic theological institutions were required to sign an oath that they would teach in accordance with the dictates of the Magisterium. Pronouncements by Catholic scholars on sexual or political matters are monitored by Rome with care and action is taken to stop them speaking where this is considered necessary. New appointments to Bishoprics sometimes seem to be dependent on conformity with the official line, and even existing bishops can be removed if they step out of line (as has occurred recently in Australia, France, Germany and elsewhere).

This might be acceptable if there was assurance that the Magisterium has the Truth, but there is reason to doubt this claim. The key presupposition of Veritatis Splendour is that the Roman Catholic Magisterium has a unique teaching role. Certainly, individuals should be encouraged to listen to the views of influential theologians and bishops. Such views need to be taken seriously, but the important issue here is whether or not these views are true. Asserting that they *are* true is not a satisfactory way of demonstrating, even in a very loud voice, that this is the case.

In recent years the Catholic Church and Pope John Paul II have given a bold and visionary lead in key areas, not least in the area of social justice and by challenging the material culture which is so widely accepted. However, when the Church imposes rules and backs them with strong language then, in so doing, it may be thought to be depriving its followers of freedom. This is not being faithful to the mainstream Catholic tradition which has emphasised, in the last analysis, the centrality of conscience, the individual alone before God.

Having sought to exercise what St Ignatius of Loyola termed 'discernment' and having taken account of Church teachings, the individual is required to take responsibility before God for his or her actions. This, in practice, is the way in which many faithful Catholics and many priests faced with specific pastoral situation behave. However, the freedom this gives to an individual to be responsible for living in truth before God can be threatening to the institution. It is not, therefore, surprising that institutional religion sometimes wishes to restrict this freedom. Havel's radical message is that to go along with such impositions is a moral failure for which individuals have to be accountable. Freedom is too high a gift to be given away without taking responsibility for doing so.

Even Cardinal Ratzinger, who is regarded by many today as one of the most conservative figures in the Catholic hierarchy, has emphasised the supreme position of individual conscience, of the individual before God:

Here is the opinion of the theological school of the Carmelites at Salamonica: 'Conscience is ever to be obeyed whether it tells truly or erroneously, and that, whether the error is the fault of the person thus erring or not.' This opinion, they say, is certain and it was held by St Bonanventure, Cajetan, Vasquez and others. Newman adds an important comment: 'If a man is culpable in being in error, which he might have escaped had he been more earnest, for that error he is answerable to God, but still he must act according to that error while he is in it, because he in full sincerity thinks that error to be truth.' ... Busenbaum, a Jesuit, has this to say: 'A heretic, as long as he believes his sect to be more or equally deserving of belief, has no obligation to believe (in the Church.)' ... The French Dominican, Natalis Alexander, wrote: 'If, in the judgment of conscience, a man is persuaded that what his superior commands is displeasing to God, he is bound not to obey.'[15]

Although the above examples focus on the Catholic Church, other religious institutions such as militant Islam, militant Judaism and fundamentalist Hinduism and Christianity are far worse. Many of these have no commitment to philosophy as part of a search for truth. The Catholic Church has been willing to accept that many of the claims it made in the past were mistaken. It clearly recognises the importance of truth and accepts that it can be fallible. It is far more difficult for this to be done in, say, Islam where the Koran is held to be divinely dictated. If this is the case, even the scope for interpretation of the Koranic text may be extremely limited and the scope for fundamentalism becomes greater. When any single text is given absolute status (as happens with some evangelical Protestants and their treatment of the Bible) the door is readily open for fundamentalism to emerge because such people will not need to seek for truth — they are sure they have already found it.

A Jesuit friend of mine put it like this:

The acceptance of doubt is the driving force of the human spirit. Faith is not faith if it thinks it is certainty. Faith within a community of faith has to remain faith despite the constant temptation to certainty. Faith liberates, where the search for certainty imprisons. It would be easy to say that the great temptation of the Catholic Church is the search for certainty — but in fact what is specific is the attempt to root that certainty in magisterial utterances. Other churches go for certainty in Scripture or 'tradition' (which usually means something other than living tradition, and often refers to how things used to be done/what used to be believed in some mythical golden age). Elements within the Anglican Church seem to be trying to find certainty in Synodical government, which as an attempt at least has a self-destruct mechanism built into it. Bureaucracies love certainties, and the faith that God preserves the Church from serious error can be twisted into a belief that if the bureaucracy says it, it must be true.[16]

The search for truth and being free to be accountable to ultimate Truth is of fundamental importance to what it is to be human. As soon as any organisation, political or religious, seeks to impose truth and to deprive people of this freedom it needs to be resisted — no matter what the cost.

Any religious, ethical or political system is likely to be more or less a construct, and any construct must take second place to an ultimate duty to absolute truth, if, of course, such a Truth is held to exist. If this is not accepted, then ethics and social norms are the highest ideals to which human beings can aspire and conformity to these should be the ultimate aim. The comfort zone of convention is then a safe place to be because there is nothing higher. Havel, Kierkegaard and the Kotzker maintain that there is something more.

To find this 'something more' means returning to the ideas of perspicuity, to development of discernment and a good conscience, to the search for wisdom and understanding. These may be found in those who are simple and unlearned more than in the clever and supposedly intelligent. It is likely to be found among those who agonise and doubt, who search and seek and who may be in confusion. Where it is unlikely to be found is in the religious fundamentalists who are so sure that they know. Not only may such people not have done any really serious philosophic thinking, not only are their claims based on the thinnest of grounds but more than this, they are dangerous because they are so satisfied that they impose their satisfaction on others on the flimsiest of grounds. As the Spanish philosopher Unamuno put it:

> Those who believe they believe in God
> But without passion in their hearts
> Without anguish of mind,
> Without uncertainty
> Without doubt
> Even at times without despair
> Believe only in the idea of God
> Not in God himself.

Vaclav Umlauf maintains that in living a life of integrity, in living in the Truth, three factors need to be balanced, and the individual needs to live in the centre of a triangle formed by these three. They are:

1. *Conscience.* For the religious believer this may mean living *Coram Deo*, before God, and being willing to account to God for everything one does. It also means developing discernment so that one can separate the true from the false.
2. *Inner dialogue.* Each individual needs to engage in an inner dialogue with him or herself, in which they will interrogate themselves about their motives and reasons for actions. This comes close to the idea of 'knowing oneself', to which reference has already been made.
3. *Concern for one's 'good name'.* By our conduct in life, we create ourselves, and we should be concerned with who we become. This is not to be determined by reputation or by what other people think of us, but it does mean living our life in such a way that it can bear examination.

There is no suggestion that 'living in the Truth' is easy nor is it simple to know what this will require in a particular situation. However, the willingness to wrestle with these dilemmas is precisely what living in the Truth requires.

JESUS BEFORE PONTIUS PILATE

When Jesus appeared before the Roman Governor, Pontius Pilate, he was asked the question which forms the title of this book, 'What is truth?'. It is a reasonable and a very fair question that has been asked by philosophers down the centuries. Jesus, however, gave no reply at all and his enigmatic silence has challenged many. Was it simply that he could not answer? What answer might he have given?

It is easy to say that truth does not exist and Pilate might well stand for the many sincere people who have despaired of truth, not from malice or from lack of thought but simply because they are unable to see a way forward. The plausibility of truth being relative seems so great. However, Jesus claimed not that he knew the Truth, but that he was the Truth. This is a very odd claim and goes completely against the way we normally understand truth. It moves attention entirely away from a rational, propositional approach to concentration on the person of Jesus himself. Of course, there are differences of opinion as to who Jesus was:

1. Christians claim that Jesus was God himself, the incarnation of the word of God,
2. Muslims claim Jesus was a prophet sent by God, born of a virgin mother.
3. Jews see Jesus as a teacher but no more than this.
4. Some modern Biblical scholars say that he was a zealot, a wandering prophet or a member of the Quran community, and that many of the stories told about him were fabricated or built up through an oral tradition that served to magnify his personality.

The Christian claim is that Jesus was the Truth in that he lived the Truth, that is, he lived a life of obedience and dedication to God. This fits in entirely with the understanding of the approach to truth suggested in this book. There is a need to move away from a propositional way of looking at truth and instead come to see that 'living truthfully' is a possibility open to every woman and man. It is to live a life responsible to God or whatever we consider ultimate, and to measure all our thoughts and deeds against our responsibility to this reality. Seen in this way, Pilate's question is reasonable and so was the silence of Jesus. If Jesus was the Truth and Pilate, standing before him, could not recognise it, then there was nothing that could be done. Jesus was an ambiguous figure; Pilate had to make up his own mind.

The same happened throughout Jesus' ministry. Even at its commencement, John the Baptist's disciples were sent by John who was in prison to ask Jesus if he was the Messiah promised by God or were they to look for someone else. It would seem reasonable to expect Jesus to have claimed the status John's disciples wished to give him, but instead he told them that John must make up his own mind and sent them back to John with no more than reports of what they had seen.

When the Devil tempted Jesus in the wilderness, one of the temptations was that Jesus should perform 'magic tricks' to prove his status. Again, he refused, preferring to remain ambiguous so that people had to decide for themselves about his identity. The same happened when he asked his own followers who people said that he was and then asked them for their views.

Jesus called his followers to 'follow me'. He did not found a band of learned academics to whom he imparted secret knowledge of the Truth that no-one else had access to (the Gnostics were an example of this approach). Instead, he called people, young and old, rich and poor, slave and free, male and female, to follow him by living in the Truth responsible to God. This call is as relevant today as it has been for more than two thousand years, and it is a call that confronts every individual. The demand is not to learn more so that we can become more clever, it is to learn to live in a way that will make us good, that will make us better people, that will transform us into something other than we are at present. This is what perspicuity, insight or the search for wisdom involves. It requires knowledge of oneself.

> Slowly the thinker went on his way and asked himself: what is it you want to learn from teachings and teachers, and although they taught you much, what was it they could not teach you? And he thought: It was the self, the character and nature of which I wished to learn ... Truly nothing in the world has occupied my thoughts as much as the Self, this riddle, that I live, that I am separated and different from everybody else, that I am Siddharta: and about nothing in the world do I know less than about myself.[17]

To understand oneself, however, does not mean to understand oneself in isolation from the community and world in which one lives. Still less does it mean isolation from God or whatever may be the ultimate reality in the universe. It means coming to freedom and freedom from fear. We do not pluck our knowledge of God freshly minted out of the ether. Initially it is received from other believers, from others who have struggled down the path before us and who try to live out its meaning. At many points in our lives the example, encouragement, stimulation, challenge and support of others can help us to deepen and grow. Nevertheless, we cannot be determined by the group to which we belong. We die essentially alone. We have to learn to live in Truth and no matter how important our communities may be, this must mean exercising our individual ultimate responsibility.

BRINGING THE THREADS TOGETHER

In the film *Contact*, Jodi Foster plays a scientist named Dr Ellie Armstrong who first discovers signals from an extraterrestrial intelligence. The first signal is the number pi which is a transcendental number, a number which goes on forever and never repeats itself. So far, pi has been analysed to 50 billion places without there ever being a repetition. Then the signals take the form of Prime Numbers which are likely to be the basis of any universal language. The point of this film is clear: mathematics represent an absolute in the universe discoverable by any intelligent species. Of course, some challenge this view and say that we simply create or construct the laws of mathematics and there is no proof.

The signal, however, is not simply mathematical. Overlaid on top of it are detailed plans to build a complex structure, the purpose of which is not clear. The cost is a third of a trillion dollars and eventually the decision is taken to proceed. There is space within this structure for one person and, eventually Ellie is selected to go. She enters above the structure which rotates at incredible speed. The capsule containing Ellie is dropped into the centre of the structure and she finds herself speeding through a wormhole in space. After a brief interval she goes down another wormhole, and then another to emerge in the Vega star system. She is then placed gently on a beautiful beach where she encounters her dead father with whom she used to be very close. She realises that her father is not real and the figure admits as much. The Intelligence that brought her to this place took a form that would be acceptable to her. It explains that the universe contains countless life forms and that human beings are special and rare, capable of great beauty and sensitivity, but also of great savagery. It points the way forward for human beings to take their place among the other peoples of the galaxy using the technology that has been given to them. However, nothing is precise. This is the whole of the message.

Ellie returns through the wormholes and finds herself in the capsule in which she started. To those observing the structure and her capsule, it appeared that the capsule simply fell through and landed in the sea, with hardly any time elapsing. To Ellie, 18 hours elapsed. She is called before a US Congressional hearing, and one of the scientists who rejects her account of what happened says that she is the victim of a 'self-reinforcing delusion'. Ellie is asked whether she is familiar with Ockam's razor, a principle to which she herself has previously appealed. She says that it is the principle that 'all things being equal, the simplest explanation is likely to be the right one'. Which, her questioner now asks, is more likely:

> ... that a message from aliens results in a magical machine that whisks you away to the centre of the galaxy to see your Dad and then a split second later returns you home without a single thread of proof or that your experience is the result of being the unwitting star ... in a hoax or a delusion ...

In saying this, her questioner is echoing the Scottish philosopher David Hume who maintained that it was always more probable to hold that miracles had never taken place than that natural laws should be broken. Another critic says to Ellie:

> You come to us with no evidence, no record, no artefacts only a story that to put it mildly strains credibility ... are you really going to tell us that we should take this all on faith?

Ellie replies:

> Is it possible that it didn't happen? Yes. I am a scientist I must concede that ... I had an experience which I cannot prove and I cannot explain but everything that I am as a human being tells me that it was real. I was given something wonderful, something that changed me forever. A vision of the universe that tells us undeniably how tiny and insignificant and how rare and precious we all are. A vision that tells us that

184 • THE CENTRE CAN HOLD

> we belong to something that is greater than ourselves, that none of
> us are alone ... I wish I could share that with you.

Ellie's experience cannot be proved, but neither can she deny it
happened. In many ways it is akin to a mystical experience and the
many mystics from many different religions around the world also
say that their experiences cannot be proved. They claim that the
world has a meaning and a purpose, that ultimate Truth exists and
that it can sometimes be approached more closely through mysticism, love and beauty than by rational inquiry.[1] Of course they
could be wrong, but they are willing to stake their lives on the
claim that they are right. This is an essential part of any realist
claim — that one makes a truth claim that depends on correspondence and that the possibility of error always exists. The most any
individual can do is to stake their life on the claim to truth.
Nothing more is possible.

In the first part of this book anti-realism and constructivism were
shown to pose a significant challenge to conventional understandings
of truth in the areas of religion, morality, aesthetics, literature and
history, among others. The claims to establish reference to foundations for knowledge by means of reason are not convincing, and
appeals to revelation as a ground for certainty, in the absence of some
independent criteria to determine which revelation to accept, are
similarly based on sand. Anti-realism maintains that truth is located
within language games and denies there is any ultimate truth.

In the second part, the first of two divides in the philosophic
road after Immanuel Kant was traced, passing through Hegel and
Marx, Nietzsche and Ivan Karamazov down to modern versions of
post-modernism. Philosophy along this road was seen to deny all
ultimate meaning and value, and any idea of God or any idea of
absolute justice and truth. In many ways there are parallels between
anti-realism and post-modernism, although the differences are also
significant. However, they both join forces in rejecting any idea of a
real world to which truth claims can approximate and, indeed, any
non-relative claims to truth. The challenge facing society from this
denial of traditional realist truth claims is extreme and few theologians or philosophers are facing it today.

The Kotzker was not aware of the atrocities in the holocaust,
just as Kierkegaard was not aware of the atrocities of Stalin or Pol
Pot's regime, but neither would have been surprised. Once the

power of the lie takes over, once truth is trampled in the dust and regarded of no account, then human beings cease to matter.

Where is Truth to be found? It is largely absent from university departments of philosophy and theology which have always claimed it was their primary concern, and it is not to be found in many university departments of literature, history, aesthetics or psychology. It is rarely found in politics and almost never in the media. It is still alive and well, however, among many so-called 'ordinary' people, who are in fact the extraordinary ones, and who show it not by their words but by their lives. Socrates said that he could not prove the truth of his claim that the soul was immortal, but he was prepared to stake his life on this 'if'. Similarly countless people around the world stake their life on the existence of ultimate Truth and seek to live in relation to this, even though there is no proof that this exists.

If a realist claim to truth means admitting the possibility of error, then the intolerance of any religious grouping that is not open-minded, humble and willing to be tentative in the realist claims it makes must be recognised and opposed. There is a need to stand up to those who are so certain of their beliefs that they reject others, look down on others, make them feel guilty or brand them as 'sinners'. There has been a moral failure of many in the Western world to stand against fundamentalism and to reject it. This is seen, perhaps, most clearly in Western nervousness in standing against Islamic fundamentalism because of an understandable reluctance to discuss religious views which others hold as sacred. However, when these views are used to impose suffering on others (as is clearly the case with groups like the Taliban in Afghanistan), then failure to speak out is a moral failure.

Wherever truth is, it is least likely to be found among fundamentalists, who are best avoided or approached with the greatest of caution. Islamic and Hindu fundamentalists, New Age cults, many of the new religious movements, right-wing conservative groups in the Catholic Church, some evangelical Anglicans and fundamentalist Protestants all need to be challenged and resisted. By contrast those:

- who wrestle with ambiguity
- for whom much is unclear
- who have a broad commitment to the common human search for understanding and meaning, and

- who are willing to learn from others and accept that whatever their position, they could be wrong

have precisely the marks of those who are seeking a realist understanding of truth. This is not an accident; it is a necessary consequence of the truth claims they are espousing because, if they are realists, they *have* to be committed to the possibility of being mistaken.

When we see:

- those who loudly proclaim certainty
- those who restrict the syllabuses of schools they control or use their influence so as to limit the search of young people for Truth and understanding
- those who are intent on ensuring that others believe as they do and seek to coerce uniformity
- those who claim that there is only one understanding of truth and that anyone who departs from it will be condemned or is sinful

then we need to ask ourselves where is the humility, the openness to the possibility of their own error or the error of the sects they support. If there is no willingness to concede that they may be completely mistaken in their perspective — even though it may, or may not, be one which they personally are willing to stake their life on — then the most they may claim is an anti-realist understanding of truth. If they are anti-realists, then they have grounds for certainty within their own language game, but they have no claim to absolute truth, only to a truth expressed within the community they inhabit. There is no need to take any more notice of them than of flat-earthers, those who think they are regularly abducted to Mars or those who see UFOs.

By contrast:

- the political prisoner locked up because he refuses to conform even though no-one knows of his existence
- the unregarded academic who refuses to play the 'game' required by his department or institution and instead devotes himself to care of his students, and who loses his job or fails to secure advancement because of his failure to publish
- the aged homosexual who tries to live his Christian commitment as he lovingly cares for his incontinent dying partner

- the Islamic theologian who argues that the Koran needs to be interpreted in the light of present knowledge even though this leads to a Fatwah being pronounced against him
- the Jewish rabbi who criticises the State of Israel's treatment of Palestinians in the name of justice and identifies and supports the Palestinians in their struggle for nationhood against his own people in spite of hatred and abuse
- the young unmarried woman who lives with her partner, who has had fourteen previous partners starting at the age of thirteen, who takes her faith seriously and who struggles to try to live rightly before her God
- the young man who tries to follow his God in uncertainty and ambiguity, wrestling with moral dilemmas and the challenges faced by a changing world, recognising goodness and truth in people from diverse cultures and traditions as well as those who, while within his own tradition, take a completely different stance to his own
- the dedicated English teacher who devotes his life to trying to communicate something of the genius of great literature to the young people who pass through his hands and to show its relevance to their lives, even though they rarely seem to comprehend
- the committed woman who decides against marriage and family in favour of caring for the poor, the refugees and those in prisoner of war camps in some of the worst affected areas of the world, and who has no money, no prospects and no real understanding of what religion requires or means, and
- the atheist who is tortured by the problems of the human condition, who is angry with the God whom he does not believe exists and who devotes his life to the search for understanding

may be closer to 'living in the Truth' than those who claim to 'know the Truth'. None of them may be the sort of people the world would regard as 'successful' and, in many cases, the world may pity them, but it may be the world which deserves pity. Those who are comfortable and secure may be the ones who have ceased to struggle and to strive precisely because they no longer regard it as necessary. They may be the living dead who have died as selves long before their physical death.

Where is truth? Not, it is claimed, in this book, with those who assert they have it, but perhaps it is with those who do not know but passionately seek a perspicuous understanding of what it is to be human and who then try to faithfully live this out. Socrates found this and as a result the Delphi Oracle judged him the wisest man in Athens, but he was condemned to death by the citizens of Athens because he represented a threat to the established values of their society. Truth is always an approximation. We may never have the whole story, but this does not mean that we may not have part of the story, which may mean widening our search to embrace not just philosophy but also psychology, literature, poetry, drama, art and mysticism.

This understanding has considerable implications for education. It means that any education system that fails to help individuals to think for themselves, to challenge the accepted conventions of society and to be passionate about the search for Truth is flawed. Yet in schools throughout the Western world this dimension is neglected. Education about science provides a paradigm case. Young people are taught how to handle genetic engineering and to understand the complexity of chemistry and physics, but they are hardly ever helped to think through to what end science is to be applied. In business courses young people are taught about accountancy and economics but they are not taught to think about the ends to which business works or how one measures the commitments of multinationals to staff, customers and the communities in which they operate. This represents a general failure on the part of education which is allowing dark clouds of mendacity to gather.

Those who emphasise the importance of perspective are right and they are also right that for too long a patriarchal, rational, Western view of reality has dominated and has been seen as the only way of looking at truth. As Newton said, 'I stand on the beach and play with pebbles while the whole ocean of truth stretches before me'. The ocean is still there. We may have some access to it but this access is partial and incomplete, and it may well depend on where on the beach we stand. The alternative is not to abandon the search but to seek to learn from and to listen to each other.

God's existence cannot be demonstrated, nor can the existence of any ultimate reality on which the universe may depend for meaning — which is why faith is required. Faith is a risk; it is staking one's life on claims to truth that may be false. This is part of the human adventure. To stake our lives, to decide what sort of selves we will create with the lives which we have been given. Post-modernists, at least some of them, leave us afloat on a sea of meaninglessness; they leave us without a centre. By contrast, the Kotzker, Kierkegaard, some Sufi mystics, Wittgenstein and Havel claim that beyond all apparent absurdity and chaos there is meaning, order and truth. This may or may not be the case, but it is a claim that is as sustainable today as ever in the past.

Truth is something that will not be arrived at easily but only by struggle, by searching and by a willingness to be open to alternatives. It will only be found by those who try to live the Truth and reject the easy option of living a lie. These individuals will stake their lives on the search and, with passion and commitment, seek to pierce through the veils of illusions, the masks of falsehood, the constructs of society and the self. Truth lies outside the comfort zone and the security blanket, and it may only be accessible by those who are troubled about existence and who are prepared to stake their lives on the search.

NOTES

CHAPTER 1 The implications of a denial of truth — or the claim to have it

1 Thomas Merton, pp. 155–56.
2 Felipe Fernandez-Armesto, *Truth — a History: A History and a Guide for the Perplexed*, Bantam, London, 1997, pp. 207–208.
3 See The New Testament, John 8:44: 'You belong to your father the devil and you willingly carry out your father's desires. He was a murderer from the beginning and does not stand in truth, because there is no truth in him. When he tells a lie, he speaks in character, because he is a liar and the father of lies.'

CHAPTER 2 Realism and anti-realism

1 This is an expression introduced by Wittgenstein which represents the whole rich life of, say, a religious believer, including not just the words said in liturgy, prayer, creeds, and so on, but also behaviour, outlook and all that goes to make up the person's world. Language expresses a form of life, and forms of life differ between and within cultures.
2 Principally, the Kalam argument put forward mainly by Islamic philosophers in the Middle Ages, by St Thomas Aquinas in his 'Five Ways', and in more recent times by W.L. Craig. The Cumulative case and Probability approaches of Basil Mitchell and Richard Swinburne also follow in this tradition.
3 Put forward by Bertrand Russell in his 1947 radio debate with Frederick Copleston.

4 This is particularly clear in Norman Malcolm's discussion of the second version of the ontological argument which is summarised in the chapter on the ontological argument in my book, *The Puzzle of God*, Harper Collins, London, 1999.
5 John Henry Newman maintained this.
6 Richard Swinburne attempted to argue this in his book, *The Existence of God*, Clarendon Press, Oxford, 1979.
7 *The Justification of Religious Belief*, Macmillan, London, 1973.
8 *The Coherence of Theism*, Clarendon Press, Oxford, 1993.
9 These issue are explored in more detail in my book *The Puzzle of God*, Harper Collins, London, 1999.
10 According to Calvin, 'being perverted and corrupted in all parts of our nature, we are merely on account of such corruption deservedly condemned by God ... this is not liability for another's fault.'
11 For an assessment of the reliability of the Gospel materials, see Peter Vardy and Mary Mills, *The Puzzle of the Gospels*, Harper Collins, London, 1994.
12 Examples are innumerable but would include the Crusades, the consistent persecution of Jews over nearly 2000 years by Christian popes, cardinals and bishops, the burning of heretics by both Catholics and Protestants, and regional conflicts in Northern Ireland, the Middle East and in many other parts of the world.

CHAPTER 3 Foundations without indubitability
1 Rene Descartes, *The Philosophical Works of Descartes*, the University Press, Cambridge, 1970, p. 101.
2 John Locke, 'An essay concerning human understanding' in *Works of John Locke*, Greenwood Press, Westport, Conn, 1985, p. 281.
3 *A Treatise on Human Nature*, Clarendon Press, Oxford, 1960, Book 1 Part 4, p. 268.
4 Ludwig Wittgenstein, *On Certainty*, Blackwell, Oxford, 1979.
5 Ibid.
6 In Britain, 10 per cent of all those who think they are the fathers of their children in fact are not. Genetic testing kits are now available to enable children to check whether their father is their biological father, but buying these kits and testing is an activity that takes place only at a late stage.
7 Ludwig Wittgenstein, *Philosophical Investigations*, Blackwell, Oxford, 1958, section 242.
8 Ibid, section 199.
9 Ibid, section 217.
10 Ibid, para. 19.

192 WHAT IS TRUTH?

CHAPTER 4 Anti-realism in religion and morality

1 This is now being challenged at the fundamental particle level.
2 D.Z. Phillips, *Faith After Foundationalism*, Routledge, 1988, p. 40.
3 Fergus Kerr, *Theology After Wittgenstein*, Blackwell, Oxford, 1986.
4 Matthew 1:25.
5 For a discussion of Natural Law, see Peter Vardy and Paul Grosch, *The Puzzle of Ethics*, Harper Collins, London, 1999.
6 Gareth Moore, *Believing in God: A Philosophic Essay*, T. and T. Clarke, 1989, p. 27.
7 Ibid, p. 28.
8 Ibid, p. 32.
9 Unless he belongs to one of the major religious orders in which case the oath does not have to be signed.
10 Through its various evangelistic, teaching and publishing activities, St Matthias' parish spearheads the group's attempts to guide evangelicals within the diocese of Sydney by making clear the 'correct' position in regard to theological truth. The influence of this group means that they are largely able to determine what is and what is not acceptable within the diocese. This is possible because of the synodical form of government within the diocese of Sydney, which is effectively controlled by the evangelicals who are influenced by this group and ensure that its views remain in the ascendancy.

CHAPTER 6 The scene is set

1 Anti-realists maintain that there are religious and moral truths which are to be found within the community of belief. They would be quite happy, therefore, to endorse the truth of central religious claims. Many post-modernists, by contrast, reject any such claims and hold that all truth claims depend on perspective. They, therefore, reject the authority of any community in determining truth.

CHAPTER 7 Ontology and epistemology

1 Immanuel Kant, *Critique of Pure Reason*, 1781.
2 B. Magee, *The Philosophy of Shopenhauer*, 1983, Clarendon Press, Oxford, p. 119.
3 Immanuel Kant, *The Only Possible Argument in Support of a Demonstration of the Existence of God*, trans. D. Walford.
4 Immanuel Kant, *Critique of Pure Reason*, 1781.
5 Alexander Pope, *Essay on Man*, 1734.
6 These two statements are the titles of books two and three of *Religion Within the Limits of Reason Alone*, Harper Row, new York, 1960.

7   Gordon E. Michalson Jn, *Fallen Freedom: Kant on Radical Evil and Moral Regeneration*, Cambridge University Press, Cambridge, 1990.
8   Ibid, p. 76.
9   Immanuel Kant, *Religion Within the Limits of Reason Alone*, Harper Row, New York, 1960, pp. 40–41.
10   Ibid, p. 68
11   Ibid, pp. 77 and 82–83.

CHAPTER 8 Hegel and Marx

1   For one of the clearest statements of this position see Nicholas Lash, *Easter in Ordinary*, SCM, London, 1989.
2   Acts 2:42 and 4:34.

CHAPTER 9 Nietzsche and Ivan Karamazov

1   Quoted in Frederick Copleston, *Friedrich Nietzsche: Philosopher of Culture*, Search Press, London, 1942, p. 5
2   Shopenhauer has had a huge influence on the twentieth century, although not directly. However, his influence on figures as diverse as Hitler and Wittgenstein cannot be discounted. See Kimberley Cornish, *The Jew of Linz*, Arrow Books, pp. 110–17, 125–27, 130–31 and 260–61.
3   Friedrich Nietzsche, *Ecce Homo*, Penguin Classics, 1979, p. 78.
4   Friedrich Nietzsche, 'On truth and falsity in their ultramoral sense', in vol. 11 of *Collected Works*, edited by Oscar Levy.
5   Friedrich Nietzsche, *Twilight of the Idols*, Penguin, London, 1968, p. 50.
6   Friedrich Nietzsche, *Ecce Homo*, Penguin Classics, 1979, p. 272.
7   Friedrich Nietzsche, *The Will to Power*, trans. W. Kaufmann and R.J. Hollingdale, Weindenfeld and Nicholson, London, 1968, p. 559–60.
8   Friedrich Nietzsche, *The Antichrist*, Penguin, London 1968, p. 113.
9   Ibid, p. 221.
10   Ibid, p. 225.
11   Friedrich Nietzsche, *Twilight of the Idols*, Penguin, London, 1968, pp. 45–46.
12   Ibid, p. 26
13   See Peter Vardy, *The Puzzle of Sex*, Harper Collins, London, 1997; and Richard Price, *Augustine*, Harper Collins, London, 1987.
14   Friedrich Nietzsche, *The Antichrist*, Penguin, London 1968, p. 147.

15 Quoted from 'Twilight of the Idols' in Frederick Copleston, *Friedrich Nietzsche: Philosopher of Culture*, Search Press, London, 1942, p. 172.
16 Jean Paul Sartre, *Being and Nothingness*, Methuen, London, 1957.
17 Elie Weisel, *The Night*, Penguin, London, 1981, ch. 3.
18 Ibid, p. 48.
19 Quoted by Surin's *Theology and the Problem of Evil*, p. 147 from Greenberg, 'Cloud of smoke, pillar of fire' in Eva Fleischner (ed.), *Auschwitz, Beginning of New Era*, Ktav Pub Co, New York 1977, p. 9.

CHAPTER 10 The denial of a real world

1 Willard Van Orman Quine, *Existence and Quantification*.
2 Willard Van Orman Quine, *From a Logical Point of View*, Harvard University Press, Cambridge, Mass., 1964, p. viii.
3 Mark Sachs, *The World We Found: The Limits of Ontological Talk*, Open Court, La Sal, Illinoise, 1989, pp. 33–34.
4 For example, on p. 1 of *Speaking of Objects*, he says, 'We persist in breaking reality down somehow into a multiplicity of identifiable and discriminable objects ...'
5 Peter Strawson, *Bounds of Sense: An Essay on Kant's Critique of Pure Reason*, Routledge, London, 1966.
6 Richard Rorty, *The Journal of Philosophy*, vol. 69, 1972, p. 661.
7 Ibid, p 662.
8 Richard Rorty, *Philosophy and the Mirror of Nature*, Princeton University Press, Princeton, 1979, p. 176.

CHAPTER 11 Post-modernism

1 Galilée, Paris, 1994.
2 Routledge, New York, 1994.
3 For instance the Aborigines in Australia, the Inca civilisation of South America; the Indian culture of North America, the gypsies in Europe and all that is seen as 'different'. When any of such societies attempt to affirm their own values they are economically marginalised and devalued by the media, by education and by countless other means.
4 Harold Bloom, in his book *The Western Canon: The Books and Schools of the Ages* (Harcourt Brace, New York 1994) argues for the importance of a fairly traditional canon of Western literature against the growing post-modern consensus, even though his choices of authors for this canon sometimes seems a trifle arbitrary.

5   Friedrich Nietzsche, *The Gay Science*, trans. Walter Kaufmann, Random House, New York, 1974, p. 125.
6   Ludwig Feuerbach, *The Essence of Christianity*, trans. George Eliot, Harper, New York, 1957, p. 12.
7   Jurgen Habermas, *The Philosophical Discourse of Modernity*, trans. F.G. Lawrence, Basil Blackwell, Cambridge, 1987, pp. 83–105.
8   Friedrich Nietzsche, *The Will to Power*, trans. W. Kaufmann and R.J. Hollingdale, Weindenfeld and Nicolson, London, 1968, p. 481.
9   Richard Tarnas, *The Passion of the Western Mind*, Pimlico, London, 1998, p. 393.
10 This derives from William Paley's argument for the existence of God which postulates someone finding a watch on a heath and, seeing the intricacy of design, recognising that it must have been made by a designer. Similarly, he claims, if someone looks at the intricacies of the world in which we live, they will postulate a designer — God. To say that the 'watchmaker' that is cumulative natural selection is 'blind' is, claims Dawkins, to say that the universe is without purpose or intention of goal. The only meaning is meaning which we create for ourselves. A similar position is taken by theologians such as Don Cupitt of Cambridge University.
11 Richard Dawkins, *The Blind Watchmaker*, Longman Scientific and Technical, Harlow, 1986, p. 58.
12 Richard Dawkins, *The Selfish Gene*, Oxford University Press, Oxford, 1976.
13 Richard Tarnas, *The Post-modern Condition: A Report on Knowledge*, trans. Bennington and Massumi, University of Minnesota Press, Minneapolis, 1984, p. xxiii.
14 Richard Tarnas, *The Passion of the Western Mind*, Pimlico, London, 1998, p. 401.

CHAPTER 12   Post-modernism and self-identity

1   The idea of a common human nature underpins Roman Catholic approaches to morality stemming from St Thomas Aquinas who based his approach on the philosophy of Aristotle.
2   Simone de Beauvoir, *The Second Sex*, trans. H.M. Parsley, Alfred Knoff, New York, 1954, p. 301.
3   Peter Vardy, *The Puzzle of Sex*, Harper Collins, London, 1996.
4   For instance, even today the Roman Catholic Church permits only the rhythm method of birth control, which effectively only allows a woman to make love if she wishes to avoid becoming pregnant in those times of the month when her body is least naturally inclined to do so.
5   St Suppl. 64.5 and Suppl. 81.4.

6   Grace Jantzen, 'Luce Irigaray: An introduction' in Graham Ward
    (ed.), *The Postmodern God: A Theological Reader*, Blackwell,
    Oxford, 1997.
7   Jacques Lacan, 'God and the joussiance of the woman', in Juliet
    Mitchell and Jacqueline Rose (ed.), *Feminine Sexuality: Jacques
    Lacan and the Ecole Fredienne*, trans. Jacqueline Rose, Macmillan,
    London, 1982, p. 144.
8   Luce Irigaray, *Divine Women*, Local Consumption Publications,
    Sydney, 1986, p. 61.
9   Ibid, p. 63.

CHAPTER 15   The Kotzker

1   Reb Israel, 'Master of the Good Name' (1690–1760), known by
    the acronym of his initials, Besht, or as the holy Baal Shem. He set-
    tled at 36 in the Polish town of Mezbizh where he eventually died.
    The Baal Shem Tov was the founder of the Hasidic movement and
    Mezbizh was the place where a new understanding of Judaism
    began.
2   The Kotzker was born in 1787 and died in 1859. In 1843 he with-
    drew from the world and thereafter lived in isolation.
3   Abraham Joshua Heschel, *A Passion for Truth*, Jewish Lights
    Publishing, Vermont, 1985, p. 9.
4   Ibid, p. 10.
5   Ibid, p. 97.
6   Ibid, pp. 158–59
7   Ibid, p. 164.
8   This is something that Bernard Lonegran recognised and used as
    the foundation for his philosophical theology.
9   Abraham Joshua Heschel, *A Passion for Truth*, Jewish Lights
    Publishing, Vermont, 1985, p. 166.
10 Ibid, pp. 159–60.

CHAPTER 16   Soren Kierkegaard and subjectivity

1   In fact, the name of one of Kierkegaard's books.
2   Soren Kierkegaard, *Sickness Unto Death*, trans. Walter Lowrie,
    Princeton University Press, Princeton, 1954 p. 64.
3   Ibid, p. 75.
4   Ibid, p. 96.
5   Ibid, pp. 57–58.
6   For instance, in saying that God is wholly simple, timeless, spaceless,
    immutable, omnipotent and omniscient, even though the content of
    language about God is, for Aquinas, very limited indeed. Compare

this with his theories of analogy of attribution and proportion.

7 Kierkegaard expressed his frustration with philosophers by means of a story which illustrates the power of philosophers to destroy that which many be considered to be of fundamental importance:

> About five years before the Postscript was written, it was on a Sunday, I was sitting late in the evening in a Churchyard quietly by myself. I sat looking onto the distance and suddenly heard a voice behind some trees. I did not want to intrude but felt that to move would cause more intrusion, so I sat still. There were two people — an elderly man with white hair and a child of about ten. They were both dressed in mourning by a newly dug grave. I learned that the boy was the old man's grandson and the person in the grave was the boy's father. I later found that the rest of the family had also died.
>
> The old man talked to the child about the child no longer having any father and no one to cling to but the old man who longed to leave the world, but there was a God in heaven from whom all fatherhood came and there was one name in which alone there was salvation — Jesus Christ. The old man stopped talking for a minute and then said half aloud to himself: 'I fear that this solace my son relinquished. To what end, then, all my hope, my care, to what end all his wisdom when, as now, his death in the midst of his error must make a believer's soul uncertain of his salvation, must cause the believer to leave the world in anxiety ...'
>
> Then again the old man spoke to the boy. He said that there was a wisdom which tried to fly beyond faith. On the other side of faith there was an illusory land which to a mortal eye appeared to lend a certainty higher than faith but it was an illusion in which a mortal could not live. He fell silent and then again spoke half to himself: 'Alas that my unhappy son should have permitted himself to be deceived! To what end all his learning which made it impossible for him to explain himself to me, so that I could not even speak to him about his error because it was too high for me.'
>
> Then he arose and spoke to the child in a voice I shall never forget: 'Poor boy, you are only a child and yet you will soon be alone in the world! Do you promise me, by the memory of your dead father who, if he could speak to you now, would speak thus, do you promise to hold fast to this faith in life and in death and that you will not permit yourself to be deceived by any illusion however the face of the world changes — do you promise this?' Overwhelmed the little boy threw himself on his knees but the old man lifted him up and pressed him to his heart. I was deeply moved. The venerable old man with his faith seemed to be an individual with an absolutely justified grievance, a man whom existence had mistreated because a modern speculation had made property values in the realm of faith insecure. Here I saw my task — to study the misunderstanding lying between speculative philosophy and faith. This became my resolve. After much thought

and keeping the old man clearly in mind it finally became clear to me that the misdirection of speculative philosophy and its assumed justification for reducing faith to the status of a relative moment was rooted deeply in the entire tendency of the age — in the fact that on account of our vastly increased knowledge men had forgotten what it is to Exist and what Inwardness signifies. (Soren Kierkegaard, *Concluding Unscientific Postscript*, trans. D. Swenson, Princeton University Press, Princeton, 1941, p. 211.)

When Kierkegaard understood this, he realised that if he desired to communicate anything on this point, it would first of all be necessary to give his exposition an *indirect form*. He wished to bring people to 'see' something — not to prove anything.

8   Hong and Hong, *Kierkegaard's Journals and Papers*, vol 3, Indiana Press, 1967, p. 2334.

9   Kierkegaard deals with this distinction in his book *Philosophic Fragments* under the pseudonym Johannes Climacus, trans. D. Swenson, Princeton University Press, Princeton, 1936.

CHAPTER 17   Wittgenstein and perspicuity

1   Ludwig Wittgenstein, *Tractatus Logico-philosophicus*, trans. C.K. Ogden, Routledge, London, 1922; and *Philosophical Investigations*, trans. G.E.M. Anscombe, Blackwell, Oxford, 1958.

2   All quotes from Felicity McCutcheon are from her unpublished Ph.D thesis submitted to the University of New South Wales, Sydney, 1995.

3   'Kierkegaard, Wittgenstein and nonsense', in T. Cohen, P. Guyer and H. Putnam (eds), *Pursuits of Reason: Essays in Honor of Stanley Cavell*, Texas Technical University Press, 1993.

4   Soren Kierkegaard, 1939, 24/5.

5   Job 12:12: 'So with old age is wisdom, and with length of days understanding.'; Job 12:13: 'With him are wisdom and might; his are counsel and understanding.'

6   Matthew 13:54 and Mark 6:2.

7   Luke 2:40 and 2:52.

8   Luke 11:49; Romans 11:33; 1 Corinthians 1:21 and 2:7; Ephesians 3:10.

9   Acts 7:10 and Ephesians 1:17.

10   Gareth Moore does not describe himself as an anti-realist, but I use the term to apply to him due to the arguments in his book *Believing in God*, (T & T Clarke, Edinburgh, 1988) and to the final sentence of this book, 'People do not discover religious truths, they make them'. For further references to Moore's work, see part 1 of this volume.

11   D.Z. Phillips, *Faith After Foundationalism*, Routledge, London, 1988, p. 207

12 George Lindbeck, *The Nature of Doctrine*, Westminster Press, Philadelphia, 1984, p. 74.
13 Ibid, p. 209.
14 Ibid, p. 211.
15 Ibid, p. 65.
16 D.Z. Phillips, *Faith After Foundationalism*, Routledge, London, 1988, p. 214.
17 Ibid, p. 228.
18 Ibid, p. 233.
19 Ibid, pp. 217–18.
20 Ibid, p. 233.
21 Ibid, p. 235.

CHAPTER 18 The Sufis
1 Idries Shah, *The Way of the Sufi*, Octagon Press, London, 1977, p. 54.
2 From al-Ghalzli's *Revival of Religious Sciences* quoted in Idries Shah's *The Way of the Sufi*, Octagon Press, London, 1977, p. 26.
3 Hazrat Inayat Kahn, *Sufi Teachings: The Smiling Forehead*, East-West Publication,1996.
4 *Ibn al-Arabi by M.S. Husaini*, vol. 1, p. 38, quoted in Idries Shah's, *The Way of the Sufi*, Octagon Press, London, 1977.
5 Both these stories are adapted from the versions retold in Indries Shah's, *The Way of the Sufis*, Octagon Press, London, 1977.
6 Id.

CHAPTER 19 Vaclav Havel and living the Truth
1 I am grateful to Stewart Sutherland's insight here, in *God, Jesus and Belief*, Blackwell, London, 1984, pp. 143–44.

CHAPTER 20 Fear and freedom
1 Kings 19:10–18.
2 I am indebted to Dr Felicity McCutcheon for many of these ideas after seeing the play with her ten years ago.
3 Psalms 36:21 and 55:20; Romans 3:18.
4 Sirach 40:26.
5 Corinthians 7:1.
6 Samuel 23:3 and Sirach 9:16.
7 Richard Lovelace (1618–1656). From 'To Althea, from Prison'.
8 Germain Grisez, 'Christian moral principles', in *The Way of the Lord Jesus*, vol 1, Franciscan Herald Press, Chicago, 1983, p. 570

9 Ibid, p. 849.
10 Bernard Hoose, *Received Wisdom*, Chapman, London, 1995.
11 John Figgis, *The Divine Right of Kings*, Cambridge University Press, Cambridge, 1934, p. 56.
12 Bernard Hoose, *Received Wisdom*, Chapman, London, 1995, p. 23.
13 Id.
14 Selling (ed), *The Splendour of Accuracy*.
15 Robert Hodge, *What's Conscience For?*, St Pauls, London, p. 228.
16 Brendan Callaghan.
17 Hermann Hesse, *Siddhartha* (1922).

CHAPTER 21 Bringing the threads together

1 Within Christianity, the Franciscan tradition in particular maintains this.

INDEX

The Thinker's Guide to Evil
Peter Vardy and Julie Arliss

A comprehensive view of how we have come to see evil in the West, and where it really lies today, with extensive illustrated use of Western art, film and literature.

In a world of violence, injustice, disease and natural disasters the problem of evil is an ever-present reality. This book explores the origins of evil in both Western theology and philosophy and in Eastern traditions. It considers evil as a psychological and institutional phenomenon and explores the role of religion in resisting the temptation of evil and offering a vision of a good life.

How did Nazism arise in Christian Germany? – Do we not do evil ourselves? – In a world where millions of children starve to death every year – Are we complicit in institutional evil? – What exactly is evil?

The authors look at the way our current ideas are presented in popular film and literature, drawing on a wide range of illustrations. They confront the problem of evil in national and international affairs, in society, and in our own hearts.

> 'Here is an excellent modern introduction to the various theories which have been and are presented to explain the presence of evil in our world. From Adam and Eve, to Sadam Hussein and George W. Bush, we see how each of us is affected by evil, willingly or unwillingly. But we also glimpse how we could make the world a better place – if only we dared.'
>
> *Bishop William Kenney CP – Bishop of Stockholm*

> 'Challenging and wide-ranging ... an excellent book for anyone concerned ...'
>
> *Dr Jeremy Hall, University of Glasgow and Editor of Dialogue magazine*

AUTHOR: **Peter Vardy** is Vice-Principal of Heythrop College, University of London, and is one of the best known philosophers of religion in Britain and Australia. His Puzzle series of books published by Harper Collins have been through many printings and are available in many languages.
Julie Arliss is lecturer in religious Education at Richard Huish College, Taunton, Somerset.